God's Empowered People

God's Empowered People

A Pentecostal Theology of the Laity

STEVEN M. FETTKE

WIPF & STOCK · Eugene, Oregon

GOD'S EMPOWERED PEOPLE
A Pentecostal Theology of the Laity

Copyright © 2011 Steven M. Fettke. All rights reserved. Except for brief quotations in critical publications or reviews, no part of this book may be reproduced in any manner without prior written permission from the publisher. Write: Permissions, Wipf and Stock Publishers, 199 W. 8th Ave., Suite 3, Eugene, OR 97401.

Wipf & Stock
An Imprint of Wipf and Stock Publishers
199 W. 8th Ave., Suite 3
Eugene, OR 97401
www.wipfandstock.com

ISBN 13: 978-1-60899-859-3

Manufactured in the U.S.A.

Unless otherwise noted, all quoted Scripture is taken from the Holy Bible, New International Version. Copyright © 1973, 1978, 1984 International Bible Society. Used by Permission of Zondervan Bible Publishers.

To my father, Merle G. Fettke,
who obeyed God's call and worked for almost thirty years
in the Post Office,

to my wife, Lorraine K. "Tilly" Fettke,
who also obeyed God's call and has worked for almost thirty years
in the public schools,

and to all those God-called and dedicated laypeople
who are obedient to their call and labor for the Lord
in all places of our society

If the church is ever again to penetrate this alienated world and to claim it in the name of Christ, its only resources are in its convinced and converted laymen [sic]. There are vast areas, geographical and spiritual, which the ordained minister can hardly penetrate; the laymen [sic] are already there, and are there every day.[1]

1. Neill and Weber, *Layman in Christian History*, 22.

Contents

Foreword

ONE OF THE CENTRAL teachings of the Reformation was the "priesthood of all believers." The Church in Luther's day had lost sight of this important biblical doctrine and had resorted to a more "professional" clergy model wherein laypeople were just spectators to the things of God. Luther rejected this Catholic position and stated: "We are all priests as long as we are Christians."

The Church in the Western world is once again at the crossroads. Are we going to train, empower, and release our laity for ministry, or are we going to keep the ministry of the Body of Christ in the hands of pastors and evangelists? Possibly one of the main reasons for the lack of significant growth in the Pentecostal Church in the Western world today is this issue. The reason for the great growth in the Pentecostal Church of the Global South is an empowered laity. The ministry of the Church is the responsibility of all believers.

This book is an answer to this very important need. It is a biblical call to follow the guidance of the Apostle Paul in developing a church: " . . . for the equipping of the saints for works of service, to the building up of the Body of Christ, until we all attain to the unity of the faith, and knowledge of the Son of God, to a mature man, to the measure of the stature which belongs to the fullness of Christ" (Eph 4:12–13 NASB). Notice that the role of the fivefold ministry is to equip the laity for works of service. Dr. Steven Fettke gives us a biblical and practical response on how to fulfill this need in order for the Church to grow and be healthy.

The advantage of "giving the ministry away" to the laity is that it helps the church in the local community to be everywhere: in hospitals, offices, schools, and wherever people work. The pastor who mobilizes his or her people reproduces himself scores of times over in his area of ministry. This book will help church leaders understand and implement a course of action that will have the laity do what the church leader cannot—be everywhere in the community. As the pastor/leader trains the people for ministry, this incredible volume will guide the training material so that it will be biblically sound and hermeneutically correct.

For over thirty years, Dr. Fettke has trained thousands of students who now minister in many countries in the world. This excellent book is not only a philosophy of how to mobilize Pentecostal laity; it is a tested manual in practical theology as well. The theories in the pages of this book have been tested and implemented in large and small churches; in the Western Hemisphere and the Eastern world; in urban settings and rural villages; in the Global South and the post-modern North. They work because they are true and changeless.

I highly recommend this book for university students, church boards, evangelism committees, and pastors who are searching for an answer in how to help and train the laity in the twenty-first century.

Dr. Bob Houlihan
Southeastern University
Lakeland, Florida

Acknowledgments

I WISH TO THANK the Administration and Board of Regents at Southeastern University for granting me a sabbatical so I could work on this book. Also, this book would not have been possible without the help and encouragement of Amos Yong, Bob Houlihan, and my lovely wife, Tilly. I also want to thank Irv Ziemann, Margaret English de Alminana, Jeff Wade, Juanita Blackburn, and Mark Anthony for their creative suggestions.

1

The Role of the Laity

A N OLD JOKE COMPARES the local church to a football game: twenty-two people desperately in need of rest watched by thousands of people desperately in need of exercise. Conventional wisdom would compare the weary players with overworked professional ministers and the fans with uninvolved laity. And while it can be true that there are many uninvolved and uninterested laypeople, maybe the real reason for the laity's apparent apathy or complacency can be discovered elsewhere. Perhaps laypeople are not interested or involved in ministry because they are neither trained nor encouraged to be involved in meaningful ministry in places where they have the most influence.

A committed and faithful laity is the most obvious and most valued part of Christ's universal Church. However, modern Christian literature has largely ignored the laity as a subject worthy of close attention and deliberate study. This is not to say that laypeople have been ignored. Far from it. They are expected to attend every church service and be involved in all of the activities of the local church. Yet how they are addressed in terms of their call to serve Christ is a matter of concern. If laypeople are meant only to be extensions of the work of the professional minister, then I think the clear intention of the call of the professional minister has been missed as well as the true callings of the laity.

Far too long in too many corners of the Pentecostal tradition, churches have been organized—either deliberately or because of popular expectation—around the work of a professional minister. Local churches often rise or fall, grow or decline, based solely on the perceived energy or dynamism of a local pastor, usually a male. It is difficult to know whom to blame for this. Are pastors largely responsible? Do they demand that their preaching and pastoral ministry be respected as *the* ministry of God to the exclusion of all others? Or are laypeople responsible? Do they prefer to allow or even require a dynamic local pastor to "do the work of ministry" so they don't have to? One vivid memory of my youth has to do with the end of a particular Sunday morning service. The pastor asked a faithful older church member to offer the benediction. The older member responded, "No, pastor, that is why we pay you." Do pastors require that their ministry be followed to the exclusion of all other ministries, or do laypeople just want to write a (tithe) check to "pay" someone to "do the work of ministry" for them so they are free to deal with their own personal issues? Why does there seem to be a lack of clarity on the role of the laity in the local church and in the kingdom of God in North American Pentecostal churches?

In the Free Church tradition, the way the local church itself is organized is in flux. A dizzying array of approaches to "doing church" nowadays has many struggling to keep up with the vocabulary: seeker-sensitive, purpose-driven, convergent, emergent, emerging, traditional, missional, evangelistic, contemporary. There seems to be restlessness among North American Christians in the Free Church tradition, a certain anxiety about what constitutes a biblical church that is truly reflective of Jesus' vision for the people of God.

What are laypeople to think about all this? What is their role in God's kingdom?

Many laypeople are "voting with their feet," leaving their local churches to attend other churches or deciding they will not attend any church. Tired of mandated programs that focus only on the local church or focus only on a particular emphasis (like lively worship or a preoccupation with entertainment, or the prosperity message), they seek what is often described as "authentic" Christianity or Christian worship and service. What constitutes "authentic," however, can seem like an elusive ideal.[1]

The last two decades have been an era characterized by an emphasis on "leadership," by which is usually meant professional ministerial leadership. Phrases like "cast a vision," formulate a program, organize for change, or become the CEO of the congregation are intended for professional ministers—usually the "senior" pastor of a local church. "Senior" leaders often use grandiose titles to highlight their authority. Sometimes, the result is a kind of oppressive dominance unrelated to the work of the Spirit (cf. 1 Cor 12:27).

---

1. Atkinson, "How to Find a Church," 10. He tries to put a humorous spin on the angst over trying to find a "good" church.

This is not to say that professional ministers as truly called pastors are not needed. And grand generalizations about *all* pastors-as-oppressors or dominators is surely not fair. Indeed, God *has* called pastors by the Spirit; the issue is whether or not these truly God-called pastors are expressing their gift of the Spirit in ways that are in keeping with the intention and fruit of the Spirit in line with true pastoral ministry. Perhaps true pastoral ministry needs definition. More on that in a later chapter.

In the pages of this book, I will argue that the professional minister who is truly called by God has a vital role in training laity for "works of service" (Eph 4:12). This view sees professional ministers and laity as complementary rather than competitive. I am not interested in denigrating professional pastoral ministry; I am interested in helping pastors view laypeople as co-ministers in the kingdom of God. Professional ministers need not be afraid to "release" the laypeople to "do the work of ministry" (Eph 4:12 KJV) rather than attempt to do it all themselves.

The issue here has more to do with the way laypeople are viewed by professional ministers. Are laypeople just those who provide the funds (via the tithe check) for the local church's ministries? Is the extent of lay ministry related solely to what the laity does as volunteers in the ministries of the local church? Some laypeople have said, cynically, that the only interest their pastor has in them is in reporting numbers of them to denominational headquarters as a sign of the pastor's success, or that he is only interested in their offerings.[2] Is it not possible, instead, that the local church leaders could train and send laypeople out into the community to do "works of service" as lay ministers?

On the other hand, how may I say to laypeople that writing a tithe check for the pastor's pay as their minister does not "get them off the hook" in terms of fulfilling God's call to minister as laypeople in a world in need of their witness? In a service-for-pay- oriented North American culture, laypeople may get the impression that they might "hire" the pastor to do ministry for them much like they would hire a lawyer to do their legal work or hire a landscaping service to care for their lawn. How

---

2. In a provocative editorial for the *San Angelo Standard Times*, Jeanie Miley expresses her concern for the lack of gravitas among pastors. "I'm wondering where the leaders are who are more concerned about the people whose trust they have been given than their own selfish interests. Is there a leader whose values include integrity and truth-telling as well as winning? Have the people I'm trying to follow been tested in the hot fires of anything—tested enough to have had the dross burned away so that the gold is evident?" ("Following the Leader No Longer Safe for the Innocent," August 16, 2008.)

do pastors and laypeople find their unique place in God's plan and carry out appropriately that plan as described by the New Testament witness? I hope to provide an answer to that question in the chapters of this book.

I am quite aware that interjecting my "voice" for that of laypeople may seem presumptuous or condescending or even paternalistic. I make no claims to be *the* "voice" of the laity; however, I do wish to express a view of the laity that I think is biblical yet largely unknown to many within the Pentecostal tradition. I am hoping to awaken the imagination of laypeople to the possibility of a local church where laity and clergy are truly partners, where laypeople are not considered second-class citizens in God's kingdom. In my zeal to promote a place of justice and community for all Christians in the local church, I face the delicate task of presenting my views while not presuming to speak as the authoritative lay voice on all matters pertaining to the laity.[3] Readers will have to discern whether or not my "voice" best expresses the intent of the New Testament witness and of the witness of the Spirit, given to both laity and professional ministers.

This also means I am not the "voice" of local pastors. While I have a unique ministry as a university religion professor, I do not serve as a local pastor. In my view, the call of a pastor is one of the most difficult—if not *the* most difficult—calling in God's kingdom. Pastors wear many "hats": counselor, preacher, mediator, spouse, parent, referee, administrator, role model, life coach. They also have to juggle the local culture, various personalities among the laity, the expectations of both local and national denominational leadership, and their own sense of self worth.[4] Their "voice" is an important one to the laity; it is the pastor who has the lion's share of the load to "prepare God's people for works of service" (Eph 4:12).

I would also hasten to add that laypeople are not objects to be studied under a microscope or items to be manipulated—no matter how "pure" one's intentions. The laity must be viewed as the living, breathing essence of the Body of Christ. Their voice must be heard even as they

3. Miller, "Newman on the Voice of the Laity," 16–31. To illustrate the possible *hubris* in claims to "speak" for the laity I refer to Edward Miller's analysis of the view of Catholic laity by the venerable Catholic scholar John Henry Newman. Miller points out that while Newman wanted the Catholic bishops and even the Vatican to "hear" what Catholic laypeople were saying about their faith and their local parishes and how official church doctrine fitted their experience, he also wished to limit their role in the local parish, denying, for instance, that they may teach theology, among other things.

4. An excellent case made for a pastor having "multiple kinds of intelligence, abstract and practical." (Dykstra, "Imagination and the Pastoral Life," 26–31.)

are being "trained" by the called pastor for the work of ministry. The pastor might have important insight for the work of ministry, but laypeople also have insight into how that training might best be expressed in their particular contexts. Far too long, lay voices have been ignored for various reasons. No longer can it be acceptable for clergy to presume to know everything for and about laypeople; the voices of the laity can and must be heard loudly and clearly. Wise pastors will listen carefully to what laypeople are saying, for the Spirit just might be speaking loudly through lay voices.

It is not too much to say that for some readers my proposals will sound like a *paradigm shift* of significant magnitude. If people have only known their local church as the place they attend worship services and occasionally volunteer for the choir, Sunday school, or Vacation Bible School, they are going to be shocked at what I propose should occur. It will require them to rethink the way ministry is done and by whom. It will require them to rethink the way ministry is recognized and encouraged. It will require them to rethink issues such as accountability, intercessory prayer, and who gets to be considered a "minister."

No longer will laypeople simply rely on the pastor to tell them what the Spirit is saying. Rather, they will be required to listen carefully to what the Spirit is saying and doing through *them*, and *they* will be expected and even required to speak boldly the Spirit's message.

No longer will the pastor be expected to do all the work of ministry; laypeople will understand that they are just as responsible as the pastor for doing this work. No longer will laypeople be able to view the church as a place to be entertained, or a place where they can feel good, or a place where they can selfishly get what they need and not seek to discover how they can minister to another's need.[5] Now they will have to be responsible for discovering their own ministry call—to their workplace, neighborhood, and family. They will recognize that they are called to participate in all kinds of ministry activities conventionally understood to be only the work of a pastor.

May God hasten the day when all this can occur. Amen.

---

5. YouTube video: http://www.youtube.com/watch?v=cGEmlPjgjVI. This video is a sarcastic "swipe" at the selfishness and self-absorption of contemporary Western Christians.

2

Some History

Some, like Pastor Seymour, Glenn Cook, and Clara Lum, worked full time for the mission. Others worked part time. Even the full-time staff worked on a faith basis with no guaranteed salary, and the majority of the workers at the mission were entirely volunteers. The staff featured trained volunteers who worked at the altar or in the rooms set aside for those who were seeking to be baptized in the Spirit or physical healing. They also led people into salvation or sanctification. A staff of volunteers folded and mailed the newspaper. Several others sorted the mail, helped build the mission's mailing lists, and wrote responses on behalf of the mission . . . many workers possessed organizational skills, practical skills, and spiritual skills. They took responsibility for many of the congregation's activities. They planned for the future while they took care of present necessities. . . . They helped prepare other upcoming leaders. They recruited other able staff persons. They preached, taught, prayed, ministered, evangelized, recorded, wrote, published, publicized, paid the bills, traveled, and founded churches. They were attempting to build a new network of Apostolic Faith believers. In short, they handled all the details and incidentals to facilitate both the ongoing life of a local congregation and the "event" that would become known as a worldwide revival. Furthermore, they took as their tools the latest in communication instruments—from periodicals to telephones—and they plotted their strategies using the most up-to-date mode of transportation, the streetcar. . . . The life of the Azusa Street Mission transcended its walls. Many volunteers in the congregation were actively involved in neighborhood evangelization. Some held home Bible studies in which they prayed with those who wanted a deeper encounter with God.[1]

LAY MINISTRY STUDIES

MY INTEREST IN LAY studies came as a result of a certain uneasiness about what I perceived as increasing pastoral control of local

1. Robeck, *Azusa Street Mission and Revival,* 108.

congregations. Since 1979 I have been teaching at an Assemblies of God Bible College[2] and in the late 1908s I began to notice that local pastors as well as numerous visiting pastors who were guest speakers at chapel services expressed what I considered to be an inordinate amount of control over their congregations. Their descriptions of the churches they pastored seemed to indicate that they and only they controlled the work of God and that work was limited to their local church services. In their expressed opinions, it appeared that all ministerial activity began and ended with them and their local church. Second, the denomination to which I belong—the Assemblies of God—had begun to formulate plans for evangelism in the last decade of the twentieth century. The plan became known as "The Decade of Harvest." Its primary focus was on the ministerial efforts of professional ministers. In this plan, the only mention of laypeople was in the stated goal of enlisting one million prayer partners to pray for the successful completion of other stated goals (e.g., planting thousands of new churches and enlisting 25,000 new professional ministers). Robeck has noted that at the beginning of the modern Pentecostal movement—the Azusa revival—both lay and ordained ministers were involved.[3] It was not solely a professional ministry effort.

The failure to include laypeople in the planning or ministerial implementation of "The Decade of Harvest" only exacerbated my frustration over what I had considered to be the increasing grasp for control by pastors and now also, apparently, the grasp for control by district and denominational leadership. My studies led me to write and present a paper on this issue.[4] In that paper, I included this simple yet very profound thought I had found:

> If the church is ever again to penetrate this alienated world and to claim it in the name of Christ, its only resources are in its convinced and converted laymen [sic]. There are vast areas, geographical and spiritual, which the ordained minister can hardly penetrate; the laymen [sic] are already there, and are there every day.[5]

2. Southeastern College of the Assemblies of God, now Southeastern University of the Assemblies of God—a Christian liberal arts institution.

3. Robeck, *Azusa Street Mission and Revival*, 108.

4. "Ministers According to God's Purpose." Presented at the Twenty-first Annual Meeting of the Society for Pentecostal Studies, Southeastern College of the Assemblies of God, November 7–9, 1991.

5. Neill and Weber, *Layman in Christian History*, 22.

As early as 1991, an article appeared in a national Christian magazine noting the "increasing detachment of the grass roots from the national and district headquarters [of the Assemblies of God]" . . . and noting the need to reexamine the way family life in local churches is addressed.[6] While not specifically mentioning lay ministry, the authors nevertheless noted a certain disengagement of the laity from what local churches were trying to do.

In 1990, Margaret Poloma published an article describing research she had done on the work of the Spirit and on institutional concerns in the Assemblies of God.[7] She noted that when pastors encouraged

> ". . . charismatic manifestations" [by which she meant the exercise of the gifts of the Spirit, lively worship, fervent prayer, and opportunity for testimony] the church was considered [by her] as alive and well and "the ones most engaged in evangelism."[8]

She also noted that

> . . . the institution that developed out of charisma and has been strengthened by fresh outbursts also seeks to tame and domesticate this spirit. It remains to be seen whether—and how much— charisma will rule over bureaucratic forms and regulations, or whether organizational concerns will stifle the Spirit.[9]

While she mentioned an emphasis on ministerial credentials over ministerial call as a sign of "bureaucratic forms" that hinder "charisma," I wish she had also examined the ways local pastors may have attempted to confine the expression of "charisma" to their local church services. Did the local church promote the evangelism she mentioned only in relation to an activity or program? Or was the evangelism related to the laity's workplaces or neighborhoods and their sense of call to those places? Also, while I would agree with her analysis about forces that try to tame and domesticate the work of the Spirit, I would have preferred that her study analyze the ways local churches empowered laity for ministry as a sign of "charisma" rather than just to analyze worship, the practice of spiritual

---

6. Tinlin and Blumhofer, "Decade of Decline or Harvest?" 687. At the very beginning of "The Decade of Harvest" program this article was already pointing out ways in which it had failed.

7. Poloma, "Charisma and Institution," 932–34.

8. Ibid., 934.

9. Ibid.

gifts, and prayer. In other words, just how much did the lively spiritual atmosphere engender among the laity a sense of mission or a sense of call to the workplace or neighborhood? And, if that sense of call was expressed, how did local church pastors encourage and promote that call?

In the intervening years since the previous two articles were written, an important change has developed in official statements about ministry by the General Council of the Assemblies of God.[10] This statement in official Assemblies of God documents is quite profound: "Every member of the body of Christ participates in the ministry of the church; all are called in some way to be ministers."[11] However, this statement does not go far enough. It does not describe just how laypeople might be called and how the local church might assist the laity in their callings. Instead, the statement goes on to reaffirm the call of professional ministers that laity might be "spiritually formed, trained, and led . . . "[12] While I certainly agree that professional ministers should do those very things, I was hoping that the document would address more clearly the call of laity and how the local church and its professional minister—the pastor—might assist laity in the callings. In fact, the reality is, if two representative publications fairly recently published with provocative titles are any indication, there has been an increasing disengagement of laypeople—young people especially—from local church involvement.[13] I am hoping that this book will address at least one aspect of that disengagement—the disempowerment of Spirit-empowered believers by the insistence of professional clergy control.

In this book, I do not wish to target only the Assemblies of God. As a member of and as an ordained minister with the Assemblies of God, I want to state clearly my appreciation for the encouragement provided me by various leaders in the Assemblies of God and for the honors bestowed on me by this denomination.[14] If anything, my motivation in

10. A statement on Pentecostal ministry and ordination, approved as the official statement by the General Presbytery of the Assemblies of God, August 3, 2009, http://ag.org/top/beliefs/position_papers/pp_downloads/pp_102909_Pentecostal_ministry_and_ordination.pdf.

11. Ibid., 6.

12. Ibid., 7.

13. Kimball, *They Like Jesus But Not The Church;* and Butcher, "When Christians Quit Church," in which the author talks about "Stayaway Saints."

14. I was given the Distinguished Educator Award (*Delta Alpha*) August 5, 2009, at the Fifty-third General Council of the Assemblies of God in Orlando, Florida.

writing this book is to enhance and embrace the work of the Spirit, not to hinder any true work of the Spirit. As an ordained minister myself, I certainly do not wish to do away with professional ministers. Rather, I would like people to consider that *all* people are called by God, and, in a very real sense, all should be considered ministers, not just those who serve as professional ministers. I will write more on that in a later chapter as I describe just *how* laypeople can be encouraged to seek after their call to ministry and *how* the local church might affirm and support laypeople in their callings.

This study of a Pentecostal practical theology of the laity will focus on North American Pentecostalism, using my experience in the Assemblies of God. This does not rule out other Pentecostal denominations—the Church of God in Christ; the Church of God, Cleveland, Tennessee; the Foursquare Church; or the Pentecostal Holiness International Church.[15] Using Edith Blumhofer's rationale for the Assemblies of God as a kind of lens into North American Pentecostalism—size, affluence, influence, connections with other Pentecostal groups and influential preachers, and its national rather than regional identity—I wish to try to formulate a theology for Pentecostal laity that could be implemented in North American Pentecostal churches regardless of denominational (or non-denominational) affiliation.[16] Thus, I will make occasional reference to the Assemblies of God as a kind of representative North American Pentecostal denomination, representative of what might be possible in other North American Pentecostal fellowships. The emphasis will be on praxis (practice).

Modern Pentecostal scholarship has yet to produce a thorough *Pentecostal* ecclesiology recognized generally as authoritative by larger North American Pentecostal denominations.[17] However, some fine-

---

15. Yes, I recognize the differences and diversity of Pentecostalism, a diversity that extends beyond denominational affiliations to theological, institutional, worship style, and cultural differences. I cannot hope to speak to all the nuances of these diverse groups; I can only hope that what I say (mostly) to Assemblies of God congregations might have some important implications for other Pentecostal groups.

16. Blumhofer, *Assemblies of God, Pentecostalism, and American Culture*, 2–3.

17. Melvin Hodges's *Theology of the Church and Its Mission* is an early attempt at a Pentecostal ecclesiology, but emphasized more the "mission" part of its title than the "church" part. It accepts uncritically a Free Church paradigm and does not flesh out important dimensions of the perspective of missions as the core of a self-governing, self-supporting local congregation.

Pentecostal systematic theology books have been written that provide chapters with a rich perspective on the scope of the issue of Pentecostal ecclesiology[18] and that draw a straight line from the outpouring of the Spirit to the establishment of the Body of Christ, the Church, and implications of that Spirit-formation of the Church.[19] I would urge future systematic theologians who write a Pentecostal ecclesiology to provide a clear and thorough explanation of the role, call, and place of both the Spirit-gifted professional minister and the Spirit-gifted layperson in God's church when addressing the issue of the theology of the laity. I do not pretend to do that kind of thorough work—the work of a systematic theologian—in this book. I prefer to think of myself as a "practical" theologian (i.e., one more concerned with praxis than with theory).

As a "practical" theologian, I am indebted to the work of Pentecostal systematic theologians, especially Amos Yong. I hope to use his theology of disability (no doubt a new and surprising term to some of my readers) in making my case for a practical theology of community that embraces all, including the laity, *all* the laity, as part of the Body of Christ and as called to and enrolled in the mission of God.[20] In his presidential address at the 2009 annual meeting of The Society for Pentecostal Studies, Yong passionately called for systematic theologians and practical theologians to explore further the implications of his theology of disability and the Pentecostal experience.[21] I believe his views have a very practical implication for the local church, which I hope to articulate in this book. Those who know me personally may very well accuse me of bias[22] since they know I have a severely mentally handicapped adult son. They also know I have already written about this.[23] It is an issue very near and dear to my

---

18. Yong, "Acts of the Apostles and of the Holy Spirit." Yong's work is a sweeping overview of the issues to be addressed in a thorough Pentecostal ecclesiology. I highly recommend this chapter for those interested in identifying the major issues of a thorough Pentecostal ecclesiology.

19. Macchia, "Signs of Grace in a Graceless World." In this chapter, please note especially his emphasis on community. See also Volf, *After Our Likeness*.

20. Yong, *Theology and Down Syndrome*.

21. Yong "Many Tongues, Many Senses," 167–88.

22. To paraphrase our Lord, "If any one of you is without bias, let him be the first to throw an accusation!" (John 8:7).

23. "The Spirit of God Hovered Over the Waters." Presented at the Thirty-seventh Annual Meeting of the Society for Pentecostal Studies, Duke University, Durham, North Carolina, March 13–15, 2008. Also published in the *Journal for Pentecostal Theology*.

heart. The way the very weakest in our community are treated will say a lot about how most are treated, and it will say a whole lot about their spirituality.

I will also seek to find the practical implications of Miroslov Volf's "participatory ecclesiology."[24] His call for a more egalitarian approach to the work of the Spirit in all people—professional clergy and the laity— would be more in keeping with North American social proclivities, but would at the same time prophetically call all believers to accept their responsibility for Spirit-inspired ministry in all places in this world.

The modern Pentecostal movement that started in North America at the beginning of the twentieth century has operated under the conviction that God has poured out the Holy Spirit on "all flesh" (Acts 2:17 KJV). On that famous Day of Pentecost, all declared the wonders of God, not just the Apostle Peter. Pentecostals have believed that God still works signs, wonders, and miracles, and that God calls all people to the divine mission of spreading the gospel. God can work beyond and is not limited by the boundaries of formal creeds, social and cultural expectations, denominational control, and priestly oversight. The channel of God's mighty works is through Spirit-filled people, not human ordained institutions, political systems, or even particular faith traditions. God's spirit is not restricted to a special class of Christians; *all* believers are invited to be filled with the Spirit so that they might be Christ's witnesses (Acts 1:8) in whatever place divinely assigned to them. The Holy Spirit cannot be conjured up, confined, or controlled by a special priestly caste; only the Holy Spirit must be obeyed, as the Spirit is clearly discerned speaking by the whole faith community.

Luke's account in Acts of the mighty work of the Spirit has been the *sine qua non* of the Pentecostal tradition, the foundational text of Pentecostal faith. God worked mightily through "The Acts of the Apostles," but God also worked mightily through the Spirit-filled lay-people such as Stephen (Acts 6–7). If the Spirit has been poured out "on all flesh," then *all* who have accepted God's invitation to be Spirit-filled have been enrolled in God's plan of proclaiming the gospel "to the uttermost part of the earth" (Acts 1:8 KJV). While it is true that the apostles Peter, John, and Paul worked signs, wonders, and miracles by the Holy Spirit, it was also noted by Pentecostals that Stephen "did great wonders and miraculous signs among the people . . . " by the same Holy Spirit

24. Volf, *After Our Likeness.*

(Acts 6:8). The resources of the Holy Spirit were available to Spirit-filled laypeople and not reserved solely for those called to professional preaching or missionary ministries.

It is my conviction that laypeople can also be filled with God's spirit and do God's work. The Protestant doctrine of "The Priesthood of All Believers" has this foundational text: "But you are a chosen people, a royal priesthood, a holy nation, a people belonging to God, that you may declare the praises of him who called you out of darkness into his wonderful light" (1 Pet 2:9). All Spirit-filled believers are called to be priests in this world; they are all enrolled in a common mission, a common office, a common calling. Although the order of God-called people begins with apostles, prophets, and teachers (1 Cor 12:28), this same order is prefaced by the thought that *each one* is a part of the Body of Christ (1 Cor 12:27), and that "though all its parts are many, they form one body . . . and we were given all one Spirit to drink" (1 Cor 12:12–13). The Apostle Peter exhorted the recipients of his letter this way: "Each one should use whatever gift he has received to serve others, faithfully administering God's grace in its various forms" (1 Pet 4:10).

A BRIEF REVIEW

It might surprise my readers to learn that much has been written about lay ministry from the Catholic tradition, a tradition that Free Church people have long thought of as the epitome of an oppressive hierarchical system. Since Vatican II, the best minds of the Catholic tradition have produced a large body of literature related to lay ministry.[25] Using the view of the laity proposed by John Paul II,[26] Catholic systematic and practical theologians are calling for a more active role of the laity in the mission of the church. "The vision, energy, faith, gifts and expertise of laity are keys to the [Catholic] church's future."[27]

Interestingly, the modern Catholic charismatic renewal brought the gifts of the Spirit bestowed upon laity into the discussion among

25. O'Brien, "Theology of Lay Ministry," 88–95; Arulsamy. "Urgency of Promoting Lay Leadership in Emerging India," 500–13; and Collins, "Fitting Lay Ministries into a Theology of Ministry," 152–67.

26. Anameje, "Contemporary Theological Reflection on the Laity," 445–70; Akinwale, "Dignity, Diversity, and Complemenarity," 651–72; and Henn, "Identity and Mission of the Laity from the Point of View of Ecclesiology," 83–118.

27. Mannion, "New Wine and New Wineskins," 193–211.

Catholic authorities about the modern role of the laity in the parish. Although the spiritual gifts were thought to be "extraordinary," nevertheless, those "charisms" were accepted.[28] In the *Lumen Gentium,*[29] there is this key passage: "The Faithful (called 'the people of God,' those faithful who were not in holy orders) . . . are in their own way made sharers in the priestly, prophetic and kingly functions of Christ."[30] Given the long history of priestly privilege in the Catholic Church, this statement is quite profound, with implications for the work of the laity in their parishes and communities.

What might also be a surprise to my readers in the Free Church tradition is the increasing interest in lay studies among systematic and practical theologians in the liturgical (and thus usually hierarchical) Protestant traditions, sometimes referred to as "mainline" churches. A recent study of these kinds of churches by FACT (Faith Communities Today) discovered that the churches with the most "spiritual vitality" were those that spent a great deal of attention on training and equipping the laity.[31] A brief review of the literature from this tradition reveals the recognition of the need to train and equip laity.[32] One prominent effort is called "The Centered Life Initiative" and is located at Luther Seminary.[33]

Realizing the failure of liturgical churches to equip their faithful adequately, resulting in a massive loss of membership,[34] mainline churches are making concerted attempts to admit failures and have made important changes. Here is one provocative quotation about these failures and the real needs of the laity:

> The church, instead of being a resource of empowerment for
> the whole of people's lives, has become yet another competitor

28. DeMerode, "Theology of the Laity Today," 140–53.

29. "Light of the Nations," the first part of the Latin title known in English as The Dogmatic Constitution of the (Catholic) Church, a principal document of Vatican II, proposed by John Paul IV and approved November 21, 1964 by the bishops.

30. Cited in DeMerode, "Theology of the Laity Today," 145; (parenthesis in original).

31. John Dart summarized this study in the article, "Oldline Protestant Churches Feeling Their Age," 12–13.

32. For example, see the articles for and against lay ministers in mainline churches in the July 13, 2010 issue of *Christian Century*: Wood, "Called but Not Ordained"; and Wheeler, "Ready to Lead?"

33. Fortin, "Centered Life Initiative," 363–72.

34. Dart, "Oldline Protestant Churches Feeling their Age," 12–13.

for their time. Church leaders reinforce the Sunday-to-Monday disconnect by focusing on internal maintenance, church growth, and in-house programs. Meanwhile, people sit in pews of churches all over the country trying to make a connection between their experience on Sunday morning and the complicated lives they live in their homes, workplaces, and communities. But the church, instead of being a resource of empowerment for the whole of people's lives, has become yet another competitor for their time.[35]

In one study of the attitudes and understandings of mainline laity in regard to their ministry in their local church and in their local communities, less than half identified their secular workplace, neighborhood, or community involvement as places of ministry.[36]

It is not my purpose to analyze the hierarchical and liturgical church traditions in regard to lay ministry; however, much can be gleaned from the large body of work devoted to lay ministry within those traditions. While I will make an attempt to find the best proposals from among these studies, I want my practical theology of the laity to be more in keeping with the Free Church tradition, of which Pentecostal churches are usually considered a part. Although charismatic laity is found in all traditions, I will speak primarily within the Free Church tradition as I present practical ways by which an understanding of lay ministry might be formulated in the local Pentecostal church.

As a final comment here, it is important for me to note that the call for more lay involvement in ministry among mainline Protestant and Catholic traditions is commendable; nevertheless, in my view those traditions are too limited in scope. Laypeople are not just called to ministry in the secular world; they are also called to ministry within the church. Ministry in the church must not be left solely to the professional minister or some priestly caste.

I must hasten to say, however, that at the beginning of the twenty-first century there have been calls for a new kind of hierarchical structure within Pentecostalism based on a restorationist understanding of apostolic authority.[37] Those who are gifted by the Spirit to be apostles,

35. Fortin, "Centered Life Initiative," 364.

36. Vos, "Laity in the World," 151–58. See also a study from the Presbyterians by Donald P. Smith, "Shared Ministry," 338–46.

37. This "new" restorationist movement has eerily similar features to the "Kingdom Now" movement of the 1970s and the "Latter Rain" movement of the late 1940s and 1950s

the reasoning goes, are those to whom believers must submit. These allegedly Spirit-gifted "apostles" have authority to bestow gifts and do the true work of the Spirit in signs, wonders, and miracles. There is even a kind of "apostolic guild," with membership determined only by those who are part of it.[38] Those in the Free Church tradition who are unaware of this development may be surprised at its growing popularity. Thus, I realize I cannot categorize *all* Pentecostals as belonging to a Free Church tradition. However, in this book I will assume a Free Church tradition.

Studies on the laity from the Free Church tradition are sparse by comparison to the two previously mentioned traditions. Some studies complain about the unnecessary and artificial separation of professional ministers and the laity as well as the *hubris* of professional ministers.[39] Reflecting on the ecclesiology of Frank Macchia and Miroslov Volf and their emphasis on a Spirit-formed *community*, Veti-Matti Karkkainen succinctly states both the primary problem and solution in regard to lay ministry: "Not until a proper theology of the laity is developed is there any hope for overcoming the perennial problem of bipolarity of person in office *versus* community."[40]

At this time in the North American Pentecostal church, I believe there is a need to articulate a way for laypeople to respond to the work of the Spirit differently from what they may have experienced before. I

---

in North America, both of which were condemned by Pentecostal denominational authorities and Pentecostal scholarship as heretical and dangerous to the true faith.

38. The International Coalition of Apostles, which makes this claim on its web site: "The Second Apostolic Age began roughly in 2001, heralding the most radical change in the way of doing church at least since the Protestant Reformation. This New Apostolic Reformation embraces the largest segment of non-Catholic Christianity worldwide, and the fastest growing. Churches of the Apostolic Movement embrace the only Christian megablock growing faster than Islam" ("Definition of 'Apostle,'" http://www.coalitionofapostles.com/about-ica/definition-of-apostle, lines 1–4.)

39. Speaking about specialized ministries within local churches, one source notes, "Although special organizations for lay men and women often energized persons for mission action, they also had a tendency to create *laity ghettos* which set artificial boundaries for defining the role of the laity in the church." (Leonard, "Church and the Laity," 630; emphasis in original.) Another writer is quite harsh in his analysis of professional ministry: "What if a kept clergy is always a harlotry? . . . What if usurpation of place and power on a grand scale has emptied the only priesthood [the laity] of its power to bless? And what if clergy cannot give this power of the priesthood back, even symbolically, by defrocking themselves, but laymen [sic] have to come and take it?" Marney, *Priests to Each Other*, 8.

40. Karkkainen, "Spirit, Laity, Ministry," 134; (emphasis in original).

do not mean to imply that I will convey some kind of mystical and secret experience; I do wish to say that Pentecostal faith communities can be organized in such a way that *all* believers' call to ministry is affirmed, enlarged, enriched, sharpened, and directed.

In accepting the title "minister," laypeople will need the support of their faith communities. I will show that this will mean community recognition and appreciation of Spirit-inspired ministry wherever it may occur in ways that are comfortable to the congregation. Many have noted that only those matters brought to public attention usually get addressed and expressed. By public recognition and testimony *all* believers can be affirmed in their ministry callings.

My proposals will require believers to wrestle with the complexities of living the life of faith in a modern, technological, self-absorbed Western culture. Easy answers are always available to casual observers from popular magazines, "how-to" books, and simplistic formulas proposed by prosperity preachers. However, discerning the true work of the Spirit among believers requires more than casual observers. Earnest, intentional seekers—whose concern is for obedience, even if that might mean going against conventional wisdom, faddish trends, and the latest technology—discern the true work of the Spirit.

It is time for a different way of organizing Pentecostal faith communities and for understanding the Spirit's gifting and mission. Is a new discernment of the Spirit's work possible among the truly committed laity? Only time will tell if my heartfelt proposals in this book will have any influence. I strongly hope that, finally, the true place of the laity in the Pentecostal church will be recognized and appreciated.

3

Who are "the Called"? Mission, Commission, and Accountability

We need to recognize that such a sense of call [as Jeremiah had] in our time is profoundly counter-cultural, because the primary ideological voices of our time are the voices of autonomy: to do one's own thing, self-actualization, self-assertion, self-fulfillment. The ideology of our time is to propose that one can live "an uncalled life," one not referred to any purpose beyond one's self. It can be argued that the disease of autonomy besets us all, simply because we are modern people . . .

If the ideology of autonomy talks us out of our call as it talked ancient Israel out of its call, we too may settle for idolatries that feel and sound like a call. An idolatrous alternative may take the form of a moral crusade in which we focus on one moral issue to the neglect of everything else. It may take the form of dogmatic crusade, which is often a disguised form of maintaining monopoly, an ecclesiastical passion, or an echo of civil religion. These are all diversionary activities to keep from facing the yielding in obedience that belongs to all who are called by this God.1

INTRODUCTION

TILLY HAS SERVED GOD faithfully in the public schools for almost thirty years, most of that time as a guidance counselor in an at-risk middle school. Few would disagree that middle-school age is a very difficult age, especially when so many kids are being reared by guardians or grandparents or are latchkey kids with little love, attention, or supervision from a parental figure. Often, Tilly serves as a surrogate mother to these kids. Daily she deals with reports of parental abuse or neglect,

---

1. Brueggemann, *Hopeful Imagination*, 19–20.

student sexual promiscuity, pregnancy, and gang activity, along with student surliness, loneliness, threats of suicide, and exhausted teachers. In all of this chaos and despair, she prays daily for God's strength and direction, and often she senses God's spirit leading her and helping her love even the worst of the worst.

This is not to say that Tilly's only concern is ministry. She strives to be the very best in her profession. Her supervisors regularly give her the highest possible ratings for job performance. Doing a good job in all aspects of her work, even the dreaded paperwork and committee work, is also a part of her mission and witness. God-called people do not slack off on those work responsibilities that they find tedious.

Tilly's day might include kids loved, parents counseled and affirmed in caring for their kids, possible suicides stopped, potential fights between gangs mediated, lonely kids given attention, and exhausted teachers encouraged. Because kids, parents, and teachers have learned to trust her—learned that she truly cares about them—she can pray for them and recommend to them the life of faith in a place where normally such activities are forbidden. In a single day she might do more significant ministry than many professional ministers would do during an entire week. What keeps her going in such a setting? Tilly would answer this way: "It is the call of God and my desire to obey that call no matter how difficult the situation."

Not once in her experience in Pentecostal churches did professional ministers and church leaders suggest a call to the public schools; as a young person she thought only pastors, evangelists, and missionaries were called. After all, only those people were discussed in church as "the called." As an adult, she understands that God can call people to various places, including the public schools. However, Tilly has not discovered any setting in the local church in which she might share her struggles and prayer concerns related to her calling. She has never experienced a setting in the local church in which her call is acknowledged and where she is held accountable for her call.

Who is Tilly? She is my wife. She represents all kinds of people in Pentecostal churches who are called to work in the factory, medical profession, business or legal profession, and government service. Like Tilly, they also need to have their callings affirmed and their prayer concerns about their workplace ministries heard. These people may well be the only "minister" whom many of their coworkers, clients, students, or customers will ever encounter. Why wouldn't the local church want to prepare them for the work of ministry in their workplaces (Eph 4:12)?

THE MISSION OF THE CHURCH

The official statement on *mission* of the General Council of the Assemblies of God says this:

> The Church is the Body of Christ, the habitation of God through the Spirit, with divine appointments for the fulfillment of her great commission. Each believer, born of the Spirit, is an integral part of the General Assembly and Church of the Firstborn, which are written in heaven. Since God's purpose concerning man [sic] is to seek and to save that which is lost, to be worshipped by man [sic], to build a body of believers in the image of His Son, and to demonstrate His love and compassion for all the world, the priority reason for being of the Assemblies of God as part of the Church is: (1) To be an agency of God for evangelizing the world. (2) To be a corporate body in which man [sic] may worship God. (3) To be a channel of God's purpose to build a body of saints being perfected in the image of His Son. (4) To be a people who demonstrate God's love and compassion for all the world.[2]

It is my purpose to "flesh out" in this chapter the implications of this notion of mission to the world in regard to the role of the laity and of the local church. Everyone in the community, not just the professional minister, can provide an effective gospel witness. The voices (and professions) of teachers, business people, medical professionals, and blue- and white-collar workers can and must be heard. These believers are also ministers in their workplaces. The local church can be a place where their callings are affirmed, where they are nurtured in their faith, where they are trained to do the work of ministry, and where their testimonies can be expressed. These lay ministers will go to places in North American society where the professional minister cannot go, either by law (the public schools) or by social convention (the secular workplace). In those secular places they might be the only "ministers" their fellow workers or students in public schools might ever meet.[3] Often, people will never darken the door of a local church or be willing to talk to the

---

2. General Council of the Assemblies of God, "Our 16 Fundamental Truths," lines 1–11.

3. See MacIlvaine, "How Churches Become Missional," 231.

pastor, but they will listen to a fellow worker whom they have learned to trust and respect. In effect, the believer who is their fellow worker becomes their "minister."

> Positively, Pentecostalism at its best is missional, in that it believes that the Spirit empowers all believers to work actively in the world for the growth of the kingdom, in mission and witness, by encountering the cultures of this world in redemptive and prophetic ways. At their best, Pentecostals have been able to inculturate the gospel, creating truly indigenous expressions of biblical faith. The spontaneity of the Spirit so valued in Pentecostal structures creates space for new and innovative cultural expressions of the gospel. Negatively, Pentecostals today have been seduced by the institutional model of the mega-church structure, in which the growth of numbers and trappings of success become the priority of mission. Top down leadership with a professional class of ministers who administer the faith is becoming the norm in many so-called successful Pentecostal churches, but at the cost of a truly missional approach that sustains personal formation and empowers all the people of God to work in the service of the King. The emphasis on performance in these churches, in which "professional" ministers, singers or administrators service the institution, has restricted the participation of the congregation in worship and world engagement.[4]

WHAT IS LAITY?

The word for lay (person) comes from an adjective (*laikos*) of the Koine Greek word for people (*laos*). While the adjective (*laikos*) is not used in the New Testament, the noun (*laos*) is used quite often. The repeated use of "people" in 1 Peter 2:9–10—the foundational passage for the Protestant understanding of the role of the laity—indicates the people distinct from pagan Gentiles chosen by God to fulfill God's purpose in the world. The word for clergy (*kleros*) appears in 1 Peter 5:3. There it referred to the believers allotted to each presbyter or each God-called church leader. Traditionally, Protestant theology has described the clergy as those who serve as overseers of the people of God in their religious activities. These professional ministers enter into their roles as church leaders by ordination, a process involving the claim and testing of a call to preach and the affirmation of that call by public ceremony.

---

4. Althouse, review of *Invading Secular Space*, 60–61.

If the pastor (*kleros*) is called to preach to and lead the local religious community, who will be the "salt" and "light" going into the world to proclaim the gospel (Matt 5:13–16)? Of course, the answer is the laity. This is the call of the laity: as they go about their daily lives the laity are to fulfill the Great Commission (Matt 28:19–20).

> If this call [of the Great Commission] is to be fulfilled, it is necessary that laypeople should be motivated and trained to involve themselves in Christian ministry, because it is only by the laity that the church can reach the whole society through its daily occupations and secular living. They are the bridge between the church and the world to which we have an obligation to minister. The church is a corporate community in which all, not just the clergy, have a ministry.[5]

WHO ARE "THE CALLED"?

Perhaps the question of who has the rightful claim on the use of the word "minister" has become a question of power in the Pentecostal church. Some would agree with the argument that the apostles' *diakonia* (service or ministry) of the Word (Acts 6:4) would give them the right to be referred to as "ministers," whereas the seven chosen "to serve" (*diakonein*) tables (Acts 6:2) should be called servants. In other words, those who are specifically called to a preaching ministry should be referred to as "ministers," while those who have not been called to a speaking ministry should be called "servants."[6] Although all have been called to be servants (*diakonos*, Mark 9:35), the word "servant" connotes a lesser status in relation to that of the "minister" in our present social context.

While there are differences in the *function* of ministries, as Paul asserted in Romans 12:4, all Christians are gifted in their own unique ways to be God's servants, or, better, "ministers." Before Paul spoke of the different gifts Christians have, he advised that believers "not think of [themselves] more highly than [they] ought" (Romans 12:3). Professional ministers can be secure in their call to preach and not feel the least bit intimidated that lay ministers are called to be "mercy-showers" or "encouragers" or "givers." Indeed, Peter advised, "*Each one* should use whatever gift he has received to serve others, faithfully administering God's

---

5. Kanagaraj, "Involvement of the Laity," 327.
6. Palma, "Who is a Minister?" 13.

grace in its various forms" (1 Pet 4:10; italics added). No distinction is made between professional ministers (those who preach) and laypeople. On the Day of Pentecost, when people were filled with the Holy Spirit for service, the apostles were joined by a number of non-apostles (Acts 1:13–15) and *all* were filled with the Holy Spirit (Acts 2:4). When Peter explained this event in his Pentecost sermon, he said that all who would believe "will receive the gift of the Holy Spirit" (Acts 2:38), presumably also to be witnesses to the gospel.

Victor Paul Furnish has called *diakonia*

one of the vital signs of faith . . . The church as such is called to ministry; each congregation is understood by Paul to be commissioned for service. Several different kinds of evidence from his letters confirm this and provide us an idea of why he sought to monitor, maintain, and strengthen *diakonia* . . .[7]

People mentioned in various places in the Bible—Epaphroditus, Philemon, and others who were not apostles, pastors, or evangelists— clearly had some kind of ministry for which they are commended. All believers should be considered ministers/servants of God; however, for one reason or another most professional clergy seem to refuse to give permission to or empower laypeople to think of or call themselves ministers. Many laypeople might also feel uncomfortable calling themselves ministers, but the proper understanding of the term "minister" gives *all* believers a new sense of dignity and power with respect to serving God. Although spiritual power for *all* believers comes from God, people through their language and institutions bestow political and social power. The language and social construct of a Pentecostal church should reflect respect for the gifts of other believers, regardless of their identity as laity or as professional clergy.

HINDRANCES TO INVOLVEMENT IN MINISTRY

While it is one thing to make a case from the Bible for ministry for all people, it is quite another thing to convince people that they are one of the "called." Some common "resistances" to ministry among the laity should now be addressed.

James Fenhagen argues that professional ministers are reluctant to acknowledge as legitimate the ministry of laypeople. This stifles lay

---

7. Furnish, "Theology and Ministry in the Pauline Letters," 131.

involvement. He quotes Peter Rudge, who argues that the organizational style of the local church can hinder lay involvement.[8] To overcome this hindrance Fenhagen presents a "systematic" model of congregational life.[9] By this is meant a style of leadership in which the pastor teaches others how to do ministry rather than doing it him or herself.

Many have noted the "confounded comma" in Ephesians 4:12 in the KJV. Ephesians 4:11 lists the speaking gifts of the church, which I would identify as those who are called to full-time professional ministry. Then Ephesians 4:12 says they are to "equip the saints for the work of ministry" (NASB) or "prepare God's people for works of service" (NIV).[10] Instead, the KJV says, "for the perfecting of the saints, for the work of the ministry . . ." This seems to describe the duties of those with the gifts listed, rather than to indicate that those gifted were to train others to do ministry (Eph 4:11).[11]

If only the KJV is affirmed as the "true Bible," then it is easy to see why professional ministers would want to do all ministry and see the laypeople only as recipients of ministry rather than regard them as fellow ministers. Fenhagen has argued that the professional minister is called to train laypeople to be ministers. Sadly, in many places, there is a kind of "imperial" Pentecostal/charismatic ministry. The pastor or evangelist wants people to look to him for the "legitimate" ministry; "enablement is limited simply because 'ministry' is dependent on the institution and gifts of the . . . leader."[12]

Robert Worley says another hindrance to lay involvement in ministry is that the stated goals of a local church often do not reflect the intention or desire or permission of the congregation and so people will not commit to the plans presented.

> The nature and intensity of persons' involvement can be best understood by examining both congregational goals in relation to personal goals, and the use of the various forms of power to achieve congregational goals or the goals of leaders.[13]

8. Fenhagen, *Mutual Ministry*, 101.

9. Ibid., 103.

10. Ibid., 99ff.

11. Kraemer, *Theology of the Laity*, 139–40.

12. Fenhagen, *Mutual Ministry*, 102.

13. Worley, *Gathering of Strangers*, 38.

Again, Fenhagen discusses what he calls "the traditional model" of ministry, which is "non-reflective and hierarchical . . . it does not lead toward an enabling ministry since it keeps the authority and power in the hands of the clergy."[14] Many local churches are organized in such a way that laypeople are not given any political power. They do not have permission to express their views or feelings, so they learn to be quiet and learn to expect that ministry will come only from the professional minister they have hired to be the pastor.

This leads to another hindrance to lay involvement in ministry— the lack of recognition or appreciation of lay ministry among the laity itself. Perhaps this occurs because the people have been taught that legitimate ministry happens only when the professional minister is involved. Others may be afraid to ask God what their gift might be for fear that doing so would lead to the pursuit of professional ministry. My wife used to be afraid to ask God what God wanted her to do for fear God would send her overseas to be a missionary. Mission service was not dishonorable to her; she just did not want to be a missionary. She had the mistaken idea that God's call always involves professional ministry and that this ministry is unpleasant. When she discovered that she was called to public school teaching and, later, to public school guidance counseling, she found great joy in serving as a minister in her place of call.

Finally, some laypeople might be resistant to involvement in lay ministry because they just do not want to be bothered with these things. They are content to view the pastor as the one who does ministry. Having a consumer mindset, they attend church for what they decide is important and useful to them. They do not understand that all people who have become a part of God's family are enlisted in God's service with those gifts given by God. It is easier to write an offering check to pay others to do the work of ministry than it is to face the trials and difficulties that come with accepting a call. Doing so might also mean the painful task of personal transformation that makes believers better servants of God.

Two pastors met weekly on Monday mornings for breakfast to talk about their churches and their ministries. One week one pastor complained to another, "We are having trouble with bats in the church attic. When the worship starts and the guitars and drums used by the worship band get loud, the bats are disturbed, fly through an open-air duct, and

14. Fenhagen, *Mutual Ministry*, 101.

bother the congregation. We have tried everything to get rid of them but can't." The other pastor replied, "We had the same problem a couple of years ago, but solved it." "Really?" said the first pastor. "What did you do?" "Well," replied the second pastor, "We went up to the attic, got to know the bats, invited them down for the service, got them baptized and had them join the church. Haven't seen them since!"

DISCOVERING MINISTRY

The process of discovering one's ministry gift(s) does not have to begin with the local church leadership, but it should. The local church should be the place where every person can receive support, energy, and education for ministry.[15] In this regard the pastor should develop a political/ organizational style that enables people to discover their ministry potential. Also, pastors can highlight their own search for ministry and help others search for theirs. "The greatest gift a pastor has to give to another is not the right answer but the authenticity of his or her own search."[16]

All members of a local congregation can be involved in appreciating the ministry of all others. If the "ministry" is not solely the professional clergy, then the ministry of *all* laypeople needs to be affirmed and supported. Richard R. Brohom has called for the local church to have a service of confirmation of lay ministry in a way similar to how some local congregations confirm people called to professional ministry.

> Unless we are prepared to suggest that the calling of the religious professional is a higher calling than that of laity and is worthy of special recognition and confirmation, we must either be prepared to do away with the ordination of clergy or move to provide for the ordination of all Christians to their ministries of service in the world.[17]

Once an atmosphere of "every member ministry" has been established, the local church can begin to help people find their particular ministry gift(s). The work of educating people concerning their gifts exists in many forms. For instance, people can be taught that ministry gifts are not confined to the local church, but can and should be a part of people's everyday existence. In fact, one's daily work may be the ministry to which God has called him or her.

15. Ibid., 106.

16. Ibid., 105.

17. Brohom, "How Can You Believe You're a Minister?" 25.

Through sermons on lay ministry, Bible studies, and personal testimony by successful lay ministers during worship services, believers are invited to begin their search for their call to lay ministry. Special services can be planned in the church's annual calendar to emphasize such a call. Special prayers can be given in worship services each week for people who have begun the quest to learn what God's call for them might be.

In an article entitled, "Ministry in the Work Setting," Carolyn MacDougall speaks of how she experiences a call to ministry: the overall direction and use of her talents, the setting in which she chooses to use her talents, and the daily and sometimes hourly decisions that are a part of her job.[18] In elaborating on these, she discusses the joys and conflicts in her work. It is evident that she feels called to and enjoys her work. Celia A. Hahn has said, "What an exciting witness could be made if the prayers of the people voiced on Sunday mornings included thanksgivings for achievements, new technical skills, small triumphs of justice in the workplace!"[19]

The church can affirm those who feel their daily work *is* their ministry, and the church can help others who feel stifled in their present work to discover whether or not they should change jobs or correct some problem in their present work situation. A pastor might allow brief testimonies of lay ministers who have successfully navigated the journey to discovery of their gift and place of lay ministry. The authentic voices of other lay ministers are powerful aids in the process believers experience in discovering their own calling. Fenhagen suggests two ways this can occur: (1) making our own journey available to others and (2) creating educational settings in which there is both trust and a spirit of exploration.[20] People need to know that they have a community of trust in which they can express their joys and frustrations, and that other people are experiencing similar feelings. In chapter 5 I will describe what I call Spirit-enabled fellowship, by which believers might create a community of trust.

The educational settings that contain trust and a spirit of exploration are myriad and diverse. Mentoring relationships, Bible studies, internships, Sunday school classes, youth meetings, and men or women's retreats are all places where such "education" about lay ministry might occur. It is important not to confine the quest and exploration just to

18. MacDougal, "Ministry in the Work Setting," 51–52.

19. Hahn, *Lay Voices in an Open Church*, 17.

20, Fenhagen, *Mutual Ministry*, 109.

what are considered conventional settings: worship services, Sunday school, small group meetings.

Discovering ministry can also occur in the local church by way of recognizing the gifts/talents of people. Often this has meant that people acknowledge and commend others for their particular abilities, but it can also mean that the abilities of certain people are appreciated even when those people were unaware that they were thus gifted. People in the congregation can serve as a kind of sounding board in hearing and seeing what kinds of things people like to do, and they can be like assayers in recognizing others' abilities. Sometimes, people need to be coaxed and prodded to share what they are thinking or experiencing as they seek God for their callings. Wise counsel needs to be available in the local church so that people are neither coerced nor neglected. Fenhagen suggests that there needs to be "a regularized system of support."[21] By this he means that people need to be sustained and enriched in their ministries over the long haul. Consistent peer communication is necessary; it can take the form of some setting in which there are one or more believers who care, who are honest, and who can be trusted. In a succeeding chapter I will describe the vital roles of testimony and loving nurture in regard to this notion of support.

Still another way people can discover their place of ministry is for the local church to make the congregation aware of various kinds of local church, parachurch, community, and work-related opportunities that are available. People can be "matched" with some kind of ministry opportunity that is in keeping with their abilities and about which they may be unaware. Spiritual-gifts tests are available in various forms. Although these cannot replace the work of the Spirit as God brings to mind gifts and callings, these can be "conversation starters" that encourage believers to start thinking about what it is God might be doing in and through them.

In a similar way, the church community can help people to discover ways to do ministry at their workplace—ways that they may not have considered. For instance, how can people be ministers to their fellow workers when they work all day in a cubicle in front of a computer screen? Can the congregation help them to discover new and creative ways to be an example of Christ? How might lay ministers share their faith in a corporate, judicial, or public school setting where national law

21. Ibid., 107.

mandates a strict separation of church and state? Gifted ministry should not be limited to any one setting.

The local church would do well to prepare to enable people in their ministries wherever those ministries may be found. Many believers are probably doing the work of ministry in all kinds of secular settings. They can give testimony about their work and provide much needed wisdom in dealing with the potential legal dilemmas of trying to do ministry in places often perceived as hostile to religious outreach and personal ministry.

VALIDATING A CALL

When believers begin to sense their calling from God, then the local church community must affirm their ministry and affirm them in their place of ministry. Timothy was encouraged to exercise his gift, which was affirmed by the laying on of hands by church elders (1 Tim 4:14). This is a powerful way of recognizing publicly the kinds of ministries in which laypeople are actively involved, including those opportunities in their workplaces. Although Timothy was probably a full-time pastor, the model of public recognition and affirmation of a call to ministry can guide congregations in bearing witness publicly that laypeople do have a legitimate ministry gift.[22]

Jim Stockard, in the article "Commissioning the Ministries of the Laity: How It Works and Why It Isn't Being Done," proposes that a local congregation commission laypeople for ministry. He suggests five points for consideration when commissioning them.[23] The first is that the commission involves the whole congregation. "The entire congregation confirms the challenge and promises support. Thus, the whole community is concentrated on one person and his or her ministry."[24] It allows the person to write the particulars of his/her commissioning ceremony, and allows others to help him/her in its composition, thus

22. See Mary Elizabeth Moore, "Commissioning the People of God," 399–411. This article comes from the United Methodist Church tradition, but it makes a strong case from John Wesley's ministry that he practiced the commissioning of lay preachers, class leaders, deacons, elders, and superintendents. "Wesley did not see ordained roles as distinct but defined them in relation to the ministry of the body . . . The ministry of all Christians was thus central to the words and practices of the early Wesleyan movement" (401).

23. Stockard, "Commissioning the Ministries of the Laity, 72–75.

24. Ibid., 72.

allowing them to say for the congregation what support will be given and what responsibilities are expected.

The second aspect of a commissioning is that it is part of a public worship service. Stockard noted that a public commissioning is a source of power and support; it stimulates congregational concern for one another's work; it lets visitors know this congregation takes seriously the work of ministry.[25]

The third aspect of a commissioning is that it is a two-way street. The one being commissioned is given ministry responsibility, and the congregation commits to ongoing support. The fourth aspect of a commissioning is that the commission is theologically grounded. It is the Great Commission that differentiates believers from a social or political club.

The final aspect of a commissioning is that it is specific. Not only does the commissioned one need to tell the congregation the exact nature of his/her work, but the congregation also needs to know exactly how to provide the support he/she needs to accomplish the work to which he/she has been commissioned.

It is best to keep the work of commissioning as simple and direct as possible. It might be counterproductive to complicate things unnecessarily. Significance and meaning can be given to public commissioning of the laity in ways understandable to all! There can be two parts to the commissioning process:

1. What the person being commissioned promises.

2. What the congregation promises in response.

In simple yet profound ways the callings of the laity and the affirmation of the congregation can occur so that everyone understands what is happening.

In terms of the first part, the person might be asked to promise these things:

1. To be faithful to God's call.

2. To give periodic reports on her ministry through public testimony in settings made possible by the church.

3. To practice faithfully the spiritual disciplines emphasized by the church.

---

25. Ibid., 73.

In terms of the second part, the congregation might be asked to promise these things:

1. To offer training in and emphasis on the spiritual disciplines (e.g., Bible study, prayer, living a holy life, etc.).

2. To provide regular intercessory prayer for every called person in the church—layperson and professional minister alike.

3. To maintain a caring and nurturing atmosphere in the local church where both mature believers and new converts are welcomed and loved.

These promises are given by the one being commissioned, then by the united voices of the congregation in a call-response fashion led by the pastor.

The beauty of this plan is that it is easy to understand and remember, and the whole congregation is involved in some way throughout the process of commissioning. The congregation gives a strong signal to the commissioned one that his/her ministry is part of the community. The commissioned one gives a strong signal to the community that he/she is in some way involved in all ministry in and through the church. Thus, one's work life and church life are linked, as they should be, and people learn how much they need one another in this life of faith. People need the affirmation of others in all aspects of life, but especially in the work of ministry. They can better cope with life's difficulties and challenges when they have been assured that people in the church community have promised their support.

ACCOUNTABILITY

The commissioning process suggested by Stockard has an important ingredient that can help a congregation provide needed support. By writing the commissioning ceremony, the commissioned believers let the congregation know in what way they are accepting responsibility for ministry. If they do not live up to that responsibility, then the congregation can call them to be responsible to their commissioning. I use the word *support* in describing this effort because church discipline is necessary for the life of the church. After all, if the congregation has entered into a contract with laypeople in their commissioning, then it is only reasonable for that congregation to get what was promised, just as the congregation should give what it promised.

Fenhagen calls this process a "system of accountability and recognition."[26] He suggests that both the person doing ministry and the ones participating in the process write down a plan for ministry. "In this way they are establishing the norms by which they are to be held accountable [and] . . . if a job isn't done, there is a clear base on which to make changes, or if done well, to offer genuine recognition and appreciation . . . "[27] However, again, allow me to emphasize the beauty of simplicity and brevity. This "contract" does not have to be a treatise or a long, legal document. Often, just writing down on one sheet of paper one's heart for a particular group or setting in terms of a call to ministry to them can reveal one's passion and desire to please God and love those people. Grammar and punctuation don't even have to be correct! All that really matters in this is the expression of one's heart.

An important caveat must be inserted here. While it is very important for believers' hearts to be heard about their call, it is also important to have godly wisdom in this whole process. Not everybody who has a heart for something actually should be doing that thing. Someone might have a heart to teach in the most difficult public school setting possible, but if he doesn't have a college degree he just isn't going to be able to do so. Another person might want to be a lawyer who advocates for the poor, but if she doesn't have a law degree she isn't going anywhere. A committee of mature laypeople with successful lay ministries can be established who then will provide feedback and counsel to those seeking confirmation of a sense of call and a public commissioning of their call. This committee can represent the congregation in assisting those whose hearts are burning to serve God. Confirmation of someone's call by two or three mature witnesses is a good policy for any congregation to establish.

The point here is that in commissioning people for ministry the *entire* congregation accepts responsibility for ministry, not just the person being commissioned. When people fail to meet their responsibilities in ministry, the whole congregation should feel the disappointment and hurt that can occur. If a congregation accepts the credit for the fine work of one of its members, so it should share the blame for the failure of

26. Fenhagen, *Mutual Ministry*, 107.

27. Ibid.

one of its members. The erring one needs the love and correction of the church community just as much as (or more than) the one who does well needs the approving embrace of the community.

THE GIFT OF THE HOLY SPIRIT

The distinctive doctrine of the Pentecostal church is that the spirit of God is available to all who ask God to be filled so that they may be effective servants of God. A strong tradition exists among these groups to rely on the strength of God by the Holy Spirit to do effective ministry. This work of the Spirit cannot be contained in programs developed by well-meaning and successful preachers or controlled by the efforts of well-meaning believers no matter how sincere they are. The spirit of God remains unrestrained, uncontrolled, and unharnessed by any human powers. Instead, the Spirit has been given as a gift and an expression of God's love. Furnish has said,

> . . . the quickening power of the Spirit is nothing else than the enlivening power of God's love to which faith is the response and by which faith finds concrete expression in the believer's life . . . If there is any doubt about the importance Paul places on *diakonia* as one of faith's vital signs, that must finally be dispelled by his words in Galatians 5:13–14, where love's service is presented as the essence of God's law.[28]

All believers are called to submit to the unmanageable spirit of God so that they might go where the Spirit sends them and minister in love to those for whom Christ has died. No program, no matter how well conceived, could ever anticipate the nuances and subtleties encountered in the ministry of any believer or any one local church. Relying on the spirit of God will mean that believers are called to intercessory prayer, suffering for and with those to whom they are called, and believing with and for them that God might help them. It also means they must wrestle with the complexities of modern life and the mysterious work of the Spirit.

The commissioning service of laypeople can include a prayer for the Spirit's empowerment for service and a reminder to the congregation that God is present in God's servants and will help them in their work. The apostle's command to be "filled with the Holy Spirit" (Eph 5:18) is expressed in the present active imperative tense in the Koine Greek text

---

28. Furnish, "Theology and Ministry in the Pauline Letters," 133.

(i.e., "keep on being filled with the Spirit"). It is an ongoing process of being filled with the Holy Spirit daily that enables God's servants to serve God faithfully and thus fulfill God's call.

Spiritual formation is vital in developing successful lay ministry. Before the fruit of the Spirit can become evident in lay ministers, they will need to submit to the Spirit's work in developing them into faithful servants of God. The Spirit's work can be tedious, painful, and time consuming because of the pruning and purging that occurs when the Spirit enters lives. Believers might be eager to get on with their lay ministries only to discover that God wants to work on them deeply first before they can experience any significant success in their callings. Fanciful programs purchased at the local Christian bookstore might make promises of "instant" success; however, submission to the Spirit's work will mean a long process of sanctification and growth rather than instant "success."

It is one thing to be excited about being filled with the Spirit to serve God, especially in an emotional worship service; it is another thing to be faithful to God's call in a tedious job when no worship band is playing and no inspirational singing can be heard. The gift of the Holy Spirit is given so that people might praise God appropriately, but also that they might become the people God wants them to be. How can lay ministers serve their coworkers when the coworkers may be hostile, backbiting, proud, and ambitious? It is by the Spirit's work that believers overcome the obstacles in life.

Pastors and congregations should remember that the gift of the Spirit is available also in times of tedium, grief, and pain. Successful lay ministry—all ministries—will have times of great difficulty and strain. This does not mean the Spirit has departed; the gifts and callings of God have not been taken away. Believers will face hardships and difficulties, but in such times the Spirit helps them in their weakness and even intercedes for them with deep empathetic groaning (Rom 8:26–27).

What is meaningful is that the work of the Spirit in empathizing with weak believers through intercession and a sense of God's presence can itself be an example to be followed. Believers so assisted by the gift of the Spirit can in turn empathize with their coworkers as they face their own difficulties, even—or especially—those coworkers who are difficult or hostile.

A former student of mine works for a large company whose regional headquarters are located in central Florida. He told me a story about a department headed by an avowed atheist. Just under him as his assistant was my former student, "Mike," a committed Christian. Many of the other workers in the department were Christians who made known their faith by keeping to themselves during break time, having private Bible studies with each other during lunch, and prominently displaying religious trinkets on their desks. One of these coworkers contracted an aggressive form of cancer and passed away just six weeks after the diagnosis. The avowed atheist boss asked the other workers in the department for volunteers to gather on a Saturday to collect the deceased worker's things at work and at her apartment to ship to her family in another state. When Saturday arrived, only "Mike" and the avowed atheist boss showed up. He made a point of asking "Mike" about the validity of the Christian faith of the other workers who had so publicly expressed their faith but were so notably absent from this organized attempt to help the family of the deceased coworker.

It can be easy and convenient to produce a "witness" that is most comfortable to believers rather than to provide a kind of sacrificial service that may be very inconvenient and even difficult. It is important for the local church to make those believers who are interested in true lay "missions" in their neighborhoods and workplaces understand that serving others often can be difficult and may require sacrifice. If "the Son of Man did not come to be served, but to serve, and to give His life as a ransom for many" (Mark 10:45), then Christians who want to be like their Lord can understand what true service may entail. The gift of the Holy Spirit is what will remind them that true service might require personal sacrifice.

Finally, it is important to note that the gift of the Holy Spirit is no substitute for a good work ethic and a concern for excellence. Far too often some Pentecostals have thought that just lots of prayer and worship time are sufficient for preparation for all things. While I certainly do not want to discount prayer and worship, I also do not want these to become a kind of excuse for not doing one's very best. People who hope to gain the trust of coworkers so that they might serve them in the name of Christ will want to prove their worth as a worker who can be admired for the mature and appropriate manner in which tasks are completed. A concern for doing a good job is also a characteristic of someone filled with the Spirit.

A varsity public high school basketball team played against a local Catholic high school team. Early in the game the public high school
players noticed the captain of the Catholic team making the sign of the
cross before shooting a free throw. "Hey, coach," one of the players on
the bench asked, "what does that mean?" The coach's quick reply was,
"Not a thing if he can't shoot!"

THE GOD-CALLED AND THE "NECESSARY OTHER"

Kathleen Norris's description of the formation of her art speaks volumes
to those called by God.

> Art is a lonely calling, and yet paradoxically communal. If artists
> invent themselves, it is in the service of others. The work of my
> life is given to others; in fact, the *reader completes it*. I say the
> words I need to say, knowing that most people will ignore me,
> some will say, "You have no right," and a few will tell me that I've
> expressed the things they've long desired to articulate but lacked
> the word to do so.[29]

It is the phrase, "the reader completes it," that so fascinates me and reso-
nates within me as well as convicts me.

In describing this "completion," Norris uses the phrase, "necessary
other,"[30] by which she means the process that completes the "transaction" (my term) between poet and reader. As a God-called teacher, I can
become so enamored with my learning and research I can isolate myself
and become entirely self-serving in both my research and teaching. In
my selfishness I can say, "I am the only 'necessary other' and the 'others'
in my sphere of influence will just have to adjust to me." It is this attitude
that poets—and teachers and all God-called people—have to resist. The
Spirit who calls us also calls us into a community in which others are
necessary. We resist that call to community to the detriment of our call
and the Spirit's work. Here is how she describes it:

> How dare the poet say "I" and not mean the self? How dare the
> prophet say "Thus says the Lord"? It is the authority of experi-
> ence, but by this I do not mean experience used as an idol, as if
> an individual's experience of the world were its true measure. I
> mean experience tested in isolation, as by the desert fathers and

29. Norris, *Cloister Walk*, 43; (emphasis mine).
30. Ibid., 42.

mothers, and also tried in the crucible of community. I mean "call" taken to heart, and over years of apprenticeship to an artistic discipline, *developed into something that speaks to others.*[31]

It is *in the community to which we have been called* that the "transaction" among all in the community occurs. Isolated individuals may create wonderful "art," but they cannot complete their work without the necessary others, without whom the art—or ministry—will be lost.

All of this may seem obvious and elementary; however, sadly, many operate within organizations, programs, and plans and remain oblivious to those people affected by those plans. A worship leader can lead in all his personal and favorite music and be oblivious to the fact that few are participating or identifying with him or his music. A pastor can preach or lead from his own agenda and be unaware of and even uncaring about the feelings or willingness of the people in regard to what he is doing. Remaining connected to these people—these "necessary others"—is the heart and soul of our callings!

A SUGGESTED CONFIRMATION CEREMONY

As I have already noted, it is important for the congregation to affirm the callings of the church members. A public confirmation ceremony has the power to give the ones being confirmed a sense of community support and affirmation, but it also has the power to emphasize to all— to witness—that these people are declaring publicly their commitment to be carrying out the mission of the Church and that the mission of the Church is very important. At the center of the ceremony is the pastor whose leadership in the ceremony during worship services also sends a strong signal of affirmation and support. In fact, pastors who lead these ceremonies might also first preach on the call of every Christian to fulfill the mission of the Church: the Great Commission. At the conclusion of the sermon, those who have been "examined" previously by the lay committee concerning their sense of call and whose callings have received the "witness" or the "amen" from the lay committee are called to the front for the ceremony. As a part of the ceremony, they will be asked to read or recite their part of the commissioning ceremony.

Please note here that instead of having half the congregation commissioned in just one service, each commissioning service might be

---

31. Ibid., 43; (emphasis mine).

better limited to four or five laypeople at most. Limiting the number involved each time makes the ceremony shorter, it gives each person being commissioned a chance to speak, and it suggests more such ceremonies to come. This can be a monthly event with four or five laypeople commissioned each time. As the months go by, previously commissioned laypeople might participate in future ceremonies by giving a brief testimony about what the ceremony meant to them and how their lay ministry has been fruitful.

The pastor will then read appropriate Scriptures related to the idea of God's call (e.g., Eph 4:12, called to do the work of ministry; Mark 9:35, everyone is a servant; Matt 5:13–16, be salt and light; Matt 28:19–20, the Great Commission; Acts 1:8, filled with the Spirit to be a witness; etc). These passages (or parallel passages) might also be used as the biblical text for that day's sermon by the pastor.

Next, the pastor will ask each layperson being commissioned to read his/her brief statement written especially for this ceremony. Those who are embarrassed to do this in front of the congregation or who are not able to speak well (or not at all, like my autistic son) might choose someone to speak on their behalf. What is important here is for the congregation to hear the heart of those being commissioned to their ministries, to describe how they have sensed God's call to their specific place, and how much they care for their coworkers. It is a form of testimony in that it is an opportunity for them to share how God has worked in their hearts and to give praise to God for gifts and callings. The emphasis here is on "brief" statements as it is important not to drag out the ceremony and thus make everyone dread its future occurrence.

While I prefer "live" presentations of laypeople reading or reciting their statements of call, I also recognize that some larger churches can afford to record these statements on DVD so that they might be played during the commissioning service. Each person could be recorded reading or reciting a statement of call and while speaking, scenes of his/her place of call could be shown, including scenes of him/her there "in action." Special music could be added by skilled video editors, which would make for a very nice video presentation. A few presentations of call (or even several, if the commissioning service were a large group) could be played at this point of the service, leading then to the next step.

The pastor will then ask the ones being commissioned to respond with "I will" to each of these three questions:

1. Will you be faithful to God's call as you have described it to us?

2. Will you bring testimony regularly to the congregation of God's work through you?

3. Will you practice faithfully the spiritual disciplines taught in this church?

Next, the pastor will turn to the congregation and ask it to respond with "We will" to each of these three questions:

1. Will you make sure there is training in the spiritual disciplines in this church?

2. Will you regularly pray for these lay ministers?

3. Will you make sure there is a caring and nurturing atmosphere in this church where both new converts and mature believers might be welcomed and loved?

The pastor will then lead the congregation in prayer for the commissioned ones. It would be a nice gesture to have other laypeople surround and lay hands on those who are being commissioned as the pastor leads in prayer. In fact, previously commissioned lay ministers might be asked to join the pastor in this part of the ceremony. The pastor might include in his prayer a call for a fresh awareness of God's spirit as each one engages in Spirit-empowered ministry.

Finally, the service can conclude with a hymn or choruses that are appropriate to the ceremony. An especially appropriate hymn for this occasion is "Take My Life and Let it Be, Consecrated, Lord to Thee"; however, no doubt there are modern choruses or songs that would be appropriate for this occasion in place of a hymn. After the singing, the congregation might be dismissed with the benediction but with the added invitation to congratulate those who have been commissioned.

I cannot finish this section without anticipating what might happen in certain churches. It must be emphasized before, during, and after the ceremony—hopefully in clear but discreet ways so as not to upset people—that this ceremony is not a legal process by which laypeople are being "ordained" into professional ministry as happens with professional ministers in some churches with a congregational polity (e.g., the Southern Baptist Convention). No doubt, some laypeople will try to use the commissioning ceremony as a way to get IRS approval for the tax benefits provided to professional ministers. In teaching on this, in the interviews with the lay committee, and even cited (in small print) in a ceremony certificate that a church might choose to give each layperson commissioned, wise church leaders should provide clear statements that express the "lay" part of the ceremony versus the professional part. Churches will do well to specify in their literature and in public statements that the commissioning ceremony is not an attempt to give every member special tax benefits designated for professional ministers. The ceremony is only the church's way of recognizing that all believers are called to serve God in the place to which God has called them.

A GROUNDSWELL BEGINS?

I have been teaching at a Christian university for over thirty years. In discussing the issue of lay ministries with generations of students, I have learned that in their churches they have not been taught about lay ministries other than those ministries directly involved with volunteer service in their local church. They also say that they are not taught about integrating their faith with their secular part-time jobs other than to invite coworkers to a church special of some kind or to try to talk to them about Jesus.

Often, these students are confused about how they are to share their faith or they are frustrated because they do not know what to say to coworkers who challenge their faith. They usually have not considered that there might be for them a call of God to a secular workplace—they usually just complain about how poorly they are treated as part-time workers. This frustration needs to be addressed so that when they graduate they do not become full-time workers who are still frustrated. So many churches are doing a poor job of preparing members to find their place in God's kingdom, even if that might mean a call to the secular workplace. Many of these students want to serve God but do not sense any call to be a professional minister. Increasingly, they are becoming disenchanted with the idea of traditional professional ministry. Instead of choosing a ministerial major as so many did in the past, many students are now choosing majors in business, education, and psychology; however, they lack an understanding of how these majors can provide opportunities for them to fulfill their call.

For some time, Christian liberal arts colleges and universities have sought to help students integrate their faith and chosen profession through courses designed to get them to think about ways their faith impacts their secular work. At the university where I work, I have been involved in this process from the religion side of the equation. In helping to design the coursework that makes up the curriculum, I am troubled by the forces from both the religion faculty and the faculty in non-religion majors who are unhappy with each other and the choices made. Religion faculty want non-religion majors to have a thorough intellectual knowledge of the Christian faith in the hopes this will translate into Christian spirituality. Non-religion faculty want fewer required religion courses, and the courses they do desire they want to be designed specifically for their majors and focused on how to make moral and ethical decisions related to their professions.

I think the opposing opinions have valid strengths and weaknesses. It is important for students to understand their faith—faith seeks understanding—and to have and be able to articulate at least a solid rudimentary Christian theology. It is also important for students to understand how to deal with the moral and ethical dilemmas they might face in their professions. However, it is most important for students to understand that they are *called of God* regardless of their chosen profession. It is not the right intellectual knowledge about theology, morality, or ethics that is the foundation of their faith. It is their relationship with God that is most important. From this relationship with God they will begin to grasp God's mission and their call within God's mission. Once that is grasped, there will be a newfound enthusiasm for being able to articulate a clear message of faith as well as to be able to decide properly about moral and ethical issues. They need close contact with mentors in their future profession, mentors who can help them grasp what it means to be *called* to be business people, teachers, and psychologists.

What seems to be happening apart from the efforts of local churches and Christian universities is a groundswell of activity from laypeople that want to make a difference in the place where God has called them. If the Christian university and the local church cannot find ways to help them define and do that, then they will begin to find ways to do those things themselves.

BUSINESS AS MISSION

One such effort is called "Business as Mission" (hereafter referred to as BAM). While it has become a buzzword among religious missions programs led by missiologists, Christian business people themselves have taken on the task of defining BAM differently. In examining this phenomenon, I am indebted to the excellent work of C. Neal Johnson.[32] His book begins with a very revealing interview:

> The idea (of BAM) is . . . simple: It assumes that the main players in overseas kingdom work are not trained cross-cultural missionaries or NGO professionals, but laypeople who take their current expertise (whether it is teaching, plumbing, electronics, or so forth) and use it to serve people in other nations . . . I view the church as an army of missionaries sitting in the pews. My job is to utilize them . . . Some people talk about "business as mission," how we're going to use business to do mission work. That's an insult to the businessman [sic], because to him business is his mission. His mission is the kingdom of God.[33]

Johnson is careful to distinguish in his book his understanding of BAM from those of others who develop a business to get into countries where they could not enter as Christian missionaries. Sometimes those "businesses" are shams, only "covers" for covert missionary activity. Sometimes businesses claim to be "Christian" in the hope of profiting from church people patronizing their business; they are hoping to exploit the Christian part of "Christian" business.

At a conference at Lausanne, Switzerland, in 2004, made up of sixty-eight BAM activists from twenty-eight countries, Johnson described how difficult it was to come up with a definition of BAM.[34] The participants managed at the conference to find some key characteristics with which they could agree.[35] Johnson's own definition reads:

> BAM is broadly defined as a for-profit commercial business venture that is Christian led, intentionally devoted to being used as an instrument of God's mission (*missio Dei*) to the world, and is operated in a cross-cultural environment, either domestic or international.[36]

Johnson is insistent that BAM should be understood as involving legitimate for-profit business enterprises, not missions' organizations or charities disguised as businesses.

32. Johnson, *Business as Mission*.

33. Ibid., 24. Bob Roberts, Jr., as interviewed by Mark Galli.

34. Ibid., 28.

35. Ibid., 29.

36. Ibid., 28.

While the participants in the conference might have quibbled about proper definitions of BAM, what is important to me about this whole process is that it was lay led with a clear desire to fulfill God's mission as business people. It was an effort from the grassroots to define mission clearly in terms of a secular business enterprise with the goal of "the greater glory of God."[37] Johnson's book is full of insights and success stories from various business enterprises established around the world. This is an amazing resource for lay businesspeople who feel called individually to be the best businessperson and/or have the best business for the glory of God. Interestingly, Johnson speaks about call and spiritual formation in very similar ways to the ones I have articulated in this book.[38] Pastors and local churches will find a rich mine of material as they attempt to help their lay businesspeople find their callings in their communities.

Efforts similar to BAM in relation to other professions might spring up from the grassroots. It would be exciting to see Public School Teaching as Mission (PSTM), Law as Mission (LAM), Medicine as Mission (MAM—not just doctors or nurses going on short-term missions' trips but serving their communities "for the glory of God"), Factory Work as Mission (FWM), Government Work as Mission (GWM), etc. Rather than consider such professions as necessary evils in our society or places that are thought to be hopelessly corrupt (lawyers, government workers, and public schools are especially singled out for complaint), the pastor and laypeople can pray that God will call people to those places in society where they might be salt and light there. In addition, pastors and laypeople can pledge to make every effort to equip the called ones and intercede in prayer for them.

It is important in my plan that lay ministers become integrated into the fabric of the local church in regard to the callings as lay ministers. However, it would also be good for local churches to sponsor in their church building groups such as BAM and any others that might spring up spontaneously. Again, it is important that such groups not be isolated from the life of the local church and its mission; however, it is also good for them to be able to meet regularly to "talk shop" about their professions, their callings.

37. Ibid., 29.
38. Ibid., 193–213.

If the formation of BAM is any indication, perhaps this is a new wind of the Spirit blowing on the hearts of laypeople. If the role of the laity has been obscured in the local church,[39] which reduces the laity to passivity,[40] then the Spirit, free and unrestrained by human control, must descend upon open hearts willing to be called to serve God in places often relegated to and dismissed as worldly, fleshly, and devilish. The laity is working and living in places the institutional church may not enter by law or by social custom. I think laypeople are beginning to listen to what the Spirit might be saying that is different from what they might be hearing in their churches. They just might be hearing God's call to these places.

It is the daring and provocative preaching of Pentecostal ministers in the past who have insisted that the Holy Spirit cannot be controlled, restricted, or restrained. The Spirit is alive and well and working in ways that cannot be thwarted by institutions, social customs, or even well established traditions. Indeed, pioneers of the modern Pentecostal movement railed against those very obstacles at the beginning of the twentieth century. At the beginning of the twenty-first century, might there be a new outpouring of the Spirit that blesses lay ministries?

I would pray that the Spirit would continue to call and send committed laypeople to the most confounding places of North American society: public schools, political arenas, the legal profession, and the establishment media. Hopefully, pastors and local churches will begin to recognize where the Spirit is working and will join in affirming and commissioning these laypeople rather than resisting this work and insisting on only conventional paths of Christian ministry. The wind of the Spirit is blowing and no one can control the direction.

---

39. Volf, *After Our Likeness*, 227.
40. Macchia, "Struggle for the Spirit in the Church," 16–17.

4

Enabling the Disabled, Empowering
the Disempowered

*As a newly Spirit-filled believer who began attending an Assembly
of God in my small hometown in Oklahoma at age nineteen, I noticed brothers, older adults, both mentally disabled, who always sat
on the back row during church services. I noticed these men because
my aunt and uncle on my mother's side were mentally disabled and
thus I was more sensitive to their presence and treatment by others
than a typical teenager might have been. The members of this little
Assembly of God treated these men with respect, listening to their
simple testimonies, allowing them to pray at the altar and join in
church fellowship. Little did I know then how much this attitude
toward the disabled I saw at this little church would affect me when
I had my own disabled child.*

*Far from the accepting and loving attitude of the people in that
little Pentecostal church, my wife and I have encountered rejection,
condemnation, and marginalization of our son and our family in
Pentecostal churches we have attended (until very recently when
we discovered Pentecostals who love our son just like he is—thanks
"Word for All Ages" Sunday school class). We hear stories like this
from other families with disabled family members, and this attitude has been noted at other places, too.1 How can I communicate
the "truth" the disabled reveal? Yes, my son is autistic and needs
the care and ministry of the local Pentecostal church to love and
serve him and his family. He is not demonized; he is a human for
whom Christ died, qualifying him for ministry. He is also a human who "embodies" a unique mark, the image of God. If only the
Pentecostal church I have known knew how kind and helpful he is,
even though he operates on a very low level. If only they knew him,*

---

1. See Phillips, *All Dressed Up and No Place to Go.*

they might recognize a gift of "helps" (1 Cor 12:28) and appreciate
the gift he brings to the faith community.2 He is both "minister"
and one in need of ministry. Doesn't that describe us all?3

INTRODUCTION

FIVE YOUNG MEDICAL DOCTOR interns were gathered around the table of a family with a Down syndrome child, a three-year-old girl. As a part of their one-day pediatric rotation, they were given one day to learn about children with disabilities. They had been asked to rank five different disabilities as to which one they would want least for their own (future) children. They had ranked Down syndrome as least. But after spending one hour in the home with the Down syndrome child, they left feeling

> . . . grateful for the (time) not so much because it influenced their career as doctors, but because it had changed them as individuals. They had been humbled by the opportunity to come to value another human being, in this case a human being with Down syndrome.[4]

The mother of the Down syndrome child was a graduate student preparing for pastoral ministry. In reflecting on the change in values that occurred in the medical students after they had spent time with her daughter, she made this observation:

> People like the medical students [were] sitting at our table, earnest and confident and smart and accomplished. People who think that the value of a human being can be measured by salary, educational achievements and leadership positions. Who think that such success in life comes because we have earned it, and that others only need to work harder to achieve what we have, whether in matters of faith or finances.[5]

---

2. Ibid.

3. Fettke, "Spirit of God Hovered Over the Waters," 170–82. Recently, my wife and I have found a Sunday school class in an Assemblies of God fellowship where our son is welcomed, loved, and treated with great respect. We are very thankful for the "Word for All Ages" Sunday school class, Victory Church, Lakeland, Florida.

4. Becker, "An Hour with Penny," 10.

5. Ibid.

At this point it is important to note that the emphasis in this chapter will be on the Spirit's empowerment of all people, disabled or "abled." The fact that the mentally and physically challenged are highlighted only serves to point out that people who are socially, ethnically, or economically marginalized by faith communities can also occupy second-class status alongside the disabled. Not everyone in the local Pentecostal community is publicly recognized for his or her Spirit empowerment, and often the social arrangements in these communities emphasize the socially and physically powerful people.

> In contrast to . . . more traditional notions of Christian ministry vis-à-vis people with disabilities, a view of the church as charismatic fellowship emphasizes that *all* members of the body of Christ are empowered by the Holy Spirit to witness to and accomplish the works of God in the world (cf. Acts 1:8).
>
> A disability perspective, in addition, focuses on how the Spirit is the author of life out of death, of resurrection out of crucifixion, and of power out of weakness. More to the point, not only does the Spirit lift up and honor the "weaker" members of the body (1 Cor 1:20—2:4) but the Spirit also demonstrates the wisdom of God in choosing to use foolishness (*moria*) and weakness to shame the wise and the strong (1 Cor 1:20—2:4).[6]

Most of us would give mental assent—even enthusiastically—to the previous statement; however, the question remains: In what way is this statement about the Spirit's enablement socially, publicly, and practically affirmed in Pentecostal faith communities? Mental assent does not always mean practical application and real life experience.

Far too often only those who have been affirmed as "powerful" are given a kind of public and community endorsement either by social cues such as social deference shown to them or by affirmations given from the pulpit by the pastor. Sadly, the qualifications for such endorsements have been understood in terms of pleasing personality, powerful worship technique, or high economic status. The weak, poor, disabled, "strange,"[7]

---

6. Yong, *Theology and Down Syndrome*, 217–18; (emphasis in original).

7. Sadly, it must be admitted that sometimes, unfortunately, mentally unbalanced people avoid proper treatment and go from church to church trying to find a place where they can act out their unbalanced state without accountability. This is another matter altogether from the issue I am addressing here. Asking mentally unbalanced people who are disruptive in congregational meetings to get professional help before they return to church is sometimes the painful but necessary task of church leaders.

and quiet ones are often not recognized for their place in the community or in the Spirit's plan for ministry. Thus, in a sense, they become "disempowered" by the failure of the faith community to recognize publicly their important role in the work of the Holy Spirit, both in the faith community and in the larger local community of that town or city.

Might it be as simple as the incident described at the beginning of this chapter, that simply spending some time together might mean significant changes in understanding and appreciating each other and our gifts of the Spirit? I will suggest in chapter 5 the value of finding ways to express a kind of *loving hospitality, Spirit-enabled fellowship,* and *a nurturing community* as important steps in empowering those who have been disempowered by community ignorance or neglect.

Typically, in many churches, the "best" and brightest are noticed, heard, and honored. In English we have even coined a term for such people: they are "charismatic" or have "charismatic" personalities. Indeed, in the history of the Church, great men and women of God have been heralded as witnesses to the mighty working of God's spirit. Pentecostals have their own hall of fame of Spirit-filled heroes—charismatic personalities—whose exploits are well rehearsed. However, what is to be said of the "little" folk, the unheralded laity whose faithfulness is seldom recognized? Sadly, not much has been said. And even worse, what is remembered of those whose very existence is questioned by our own popular pneumatology (the understanding of the work of the Holy Spirit)—those who either don't "operate within the gifts" or those who "don't receive" the ministry of the gifted by their chronic sickness or disability? Instead of being loved and accepted for who they are, they are often condemned for their lack of faith or apparent demonization simply by virtue of their having a disability or chronic illness.

Might others also be stigmatized or marginalized simply because they are socially or economically disadvantaged? In a large Pentecostal church with a large number of wealthy and influential people, special prayer is offered for people during church services at altar benches. Trained people are assigned to pray for those who come forward. An older woman, "Sarah," known by many as very poor and uneducated, yet also known as a quiet and humble "prayer warrior" (a term applied to those who pray fervently daily for long periods of time) approached the altar benches while the trained prayer "team" was praying for someone she knew and for whom she had been praying. Immediately, a spouse of one of the pastoral staff went to her and told her to go back to her seat and allow only the prayer "team" to do the praying. Sarah humbly and quietly complied, but the message was clear: she was not welcome to express her intercessory prayer gift, even someone for whom she had been praying. Sarah was not socially or economically favored enough to be allowed simply to pray for another believer.

Thus, there becomes a kind of hierarchy of those with the "best" and "highest" gifts—and thus deemed the "best" and most "spiritual"—all the way down to those so marginalized and insignificant that they might be said to have little or no "life force" at all and thus not matter much at all. Is it possible to form a community resistant to the construction of hierarchical structures?[8] Is it possible that God's spirit is still operative even in those we most often consider as having little "life force" or social or economic influence? And, if so, should our pneumatology in regard to human activity or human influence start with conception rather than with salvation or Spirit-baptism?

Luke records the angel Gabriel making the audacious claim that John will be "filled with the Spirit from birth" (Luke 1:15). That certainly works against our common thought that the Spirit begins working in humans mostly at the "age of accountability" (a nebulous and mysterious stage of life) by the conviction of the Spirit or as described by the Wesleyan prevenient grace.[9] While John is in the womb he leaps for joy when he hears Mary's voice and John's mother is filled with the Holy Spirit (Luke 1:41). Do these passages fit with our current definitions of the work of the Spirit in the stages of human life?[10]

8. See Hauerwas and Vanier, *Living Gently in a Violent World*.

9. Prevenient grace convicts, calls (outwardly), enlightens, and enables before conversion and makes conversion and faith possible. The word "prevenient" (or, as it is sometimes written, "preventing") means coming before, preceding, or antecedent. God's grace is prevenient in our lives when it creates within us, and then prompts our spiritual desire to return to God. God's grace acts preveniently, drawing us to faith in Jesus Christ.

10. No, I am not advocating a neo-Pelagianism. I am only saying that there is inadequate appreciation for the work of the Holy Spirit in creation, making people who they are, placing on and in them the image of God, providing their "life force." This view does not rule out the necessity of acknowledgement of sin, repentance, and salvation individually decided through Christ alone. My view has more to do with recognizing the intrinsic value of humans just because they have been created by the work of God's spirit.

John's parents, who were older, were believed to be past their prime and thus of little influence in the community. God did not choose a younger, vital, influential couple through whom would come the herald of the Christ; God chose those who were no longer thought to be useful. Consider also Mary and Joseph, who were socially and economically marginalized in their society; yet God chose them as parents for the Christ. God announced the birth of the Christ to humble shepherds in the countryside, not to the powerful people in Jerusalem.

In creation God provides the animation or "life force" that identifies us individually as who we are (Gen 2:7). If our pneumatology can begin with conception and birth, then those who are not high on the hierarchy of giftedness or significance in the way normally understood can be appreciated for the way God has created them and given them their unique "life force." This is also the work of the Spirit and not God's "mistake"[11] or the product of human sin or demonic activity. This kind of pneumatology refuses to demonize and marginalize those whose existence seems contrary to a contemporary understanding of who is a part of God's good creation. In fact, this pneumatology would argue instead that God's spirit created all with their own unique "life force" that expresses God's true intention for them. Did the spirit of God "hover" over my autistic son in his conception and birth? I want very much to believe that the disabled are "marked" by God in their creation and are not problems to be solved. The disabled should be recognized as having a "life force" made possible by the Spirit's work.[12] This approach to pneumatology has great implications for those whose very lives have been defined by their disability.

---

11. Yong discusses at length attempts by some to blame God for disabilities and others to "protect" (my term) their theology and not blame God for disabilities by saying that God only "*allows*" disabilities (Yong's term and emphasis). Yong, *Theology of Down Syndrome*, 162–69.

12. About the man born blind in John 9. The story is told to highlight "the works of God" in his life as a sign that God has come in Jesus Christ; as Creator, God in Christ can "create" newness as God wills. The story says nothing about the man's intrinsic value to the believing community initially. Actually, it is when his sight is restored that the community religious leaders are unwilling to accept him or his testimony about the word of God in Jesus Christ. My point has more to do with the acceptance of folks regardless of their condition as people in whom "the works of God" are evident, both in wholeness and in sickness or disability. Disabled people also can have a testimony of the work of God in them, if for no other reason than their creation. The community can embrace that testimony of the "works of God."

Perhaps in similar but less dramatic ways than the obviously disabled, socially and economically marginalized believers, too, have been defined by their status. Their birth into poor or disadvantaged families often puts them into a "lower" class, even within the local church. Thus, again, people's value by their very creation is of paramount importance, and not whether they were born with a silver spoon in their mouth or are related to "influential" people.

CREATION AND IMAGO DEI: WHO OR WHAT ARE THE "EMBODIED" MADE IN GOD'S IMAGE?

In what ways can the work of the Spirit in creation and the resultant image of God placed on all humans be understood in terms of human experience? What makes each person a person? Walter Eichrodt calls the "image of God" (*imago Dei*) the gift of personhood. "For man [sic] to be created in the likeness of God's image can only mean that on him, too, personhood is bestowed as the definitive characteristic of his nature."[13] If God's image implies personhood, then humanity, and indeed, the Church, seems to have interpreted human creation only in terms of those considered the able-bodied. That is, does the definition of "personhood" automatically imply able-bodied and able-minded people? Or, to put it another way, is the frame of reference for both Christian anthropology and Christian spirituality only able-bodied and able-minded persons? It would seem that the able-bodied and able-minded are the lens through which these things are understood. Perhaps we need to "reformulate our understanding of what it means to be human."[14]

In a moving and compelling essay, Robert C. Anderson has made some salient points and asked some important questions:

> The discipline of theology offers humanity a powerful pathway toward discovering the mysteries and wonder of life . . . Theological discourse is intrinsically relationship driven (the nature of community: God, humanity and each other). Religious practice urges us into moral responsibility toward each other. These value-laden qualities of theological education compel us to ask the questions, "Why is theology relatively silent about the human experience of disability? Should theology have a response to this dimension of life?"[15]

13. Eichrodt, *Theology of the Old Testament*, 2:126.

14. Yong, *Theology and Down Syndrome*, 169.

15. Anderson, "Disabled Human Body in Theological Education," 41.

Anderson notes studies done on cultures that mark their people in some way (e.g., Jewish circumcision). This "marking" "exemplifies how cultural meanings convey social values."[16] While the disabled are not marked deliberately as in Jewish circumcision, they are, nonetheless, "marked" or noted for their weakness or they are marginalized by their disability and apparent lack of spirituality. This expresses a cultural decision on the part of the Pentecostal subculture. If no one can help how he or she is "embodied" in creation, including the disabled, then it seems very unjust to single out the disabled for their inability to adjust their embodiment or their alleged insufficiency in believing in divine healing.

Just how are people "embodied" and how should the Church interpret the disabled as "embodied" that way?[17] Of what "value" are they? Does God's "mark" on them also convey social value to the faith community? What social value is conveyed in Paul's expression in Colossians 3:9–11: "Do not lie to each other, since you have taken off your old self with its practices and have put on the new self, which is being renewed in knowledge in the image of its Creator. Here there is no Greek or Jew, circumcised or uncircumcised, barbarian, Scythian, slave or free, but Christ is all, and is in all"?[18]

In our own experience of our son and his condition, Tilly and I have often remarked about his potential healing as something we might actually regret. We don't mean by that to wish him ill (or be accused by some as not having enough faith!).[19] We are saying that for him to be "healed" would imply that who he is right now is of little value. And for him to be "healed" would also mean that he would not be the person we have come to know him to be in his twenty-six years of existence. Thus, he would not be the one whom God created as a person who happens to be autistic. In reflecting on her own disability, Helen Betenbaugh has said, "We are told that we (the disabled) have an obligation to be *cured* by the prayers of the church rather than *healed* by people's acceptance

16 [16] Ibid., 42.

17. " . . . the time is long overdue for a disability theology of embodiment" (Yong, *Theology and Down Syndrome*, 181–84).

18. Yes, it is referring to equal consideration for those who are saved and a part of the Church. I would argue that the passage can help us appreciate the disabled for who they are just as they are.

19. Dusing, "Trophimus Have I Left at Miletus Sick."

of us as we are."[20] Perhaps my son's condition is God's creative "mark" on him; it is his "divine embodiment." We value him for who he is in the way God has made him.[21] Here is how Nancy Eisland put it: "My disability has taught me who I am and who God is. What would it mean to be without this knowledge? Would I be absolutely unknown to myself in heaven, and perhaps even unknown to God?"[22]

It is important to note here the stigma that can attach also to those who are socially and economically "disabled." Such people might be heard to say, "If only I were more wealthy," or "If only I were prettier," or "smarter," or "If I had been born into a pastor's home," or some such expression of their feelings of being "second-class" citizens in God's (local) kingdom. Instead, how might the Church say to them, "Regardless of your looks, your family, or your bank balance, you are valued and honored in this community as a person called by God every bit as much as are the wealthy and influential."

Jean Vanier founded homes for the disabled throughout Europe and North America and named them *L'Arche* (French for "the ark") communities. In these communities of disabled and abled people, the rule was that everyone mattered; everyone was created in God's image. Rather than viewing persons—any persons, disabled or abled—as defined by their particular embodiment, Vanier believed people can be appreciated for who they are and the gifts they bring to the community. Through such a lens believers can begin to appreciate the life and gifts of all people regardless of class, condition or ability. Vanier recounts the story of a visitor to a *L'Arche* community who was put off by the happiness of a Down syndrome member of the community. Vanier pointed out that the "abled" man was totally blind to the beauty of the "disabled" man.

> Fundamentally, when people start lamenting because there are people with handicaps in our world, the question is whether it is more sad that there are people with handicaps or that there are people who reject them. Which is the greater handicap?[23]

20. Bentenbaugh, "Disability," 208; (emphasis in original).

21. Yong describes his mother's struggle with the birth and meaning of Amos's brother's life, someone with Down syndrome, " . . . Mark's life . . . would be a witness to God's larger plans for her, for him, for the family, and for others" (Yong, *Theology and Down Syndrome*, 156).

22. Eisland, "Encountering the Disabled God," 13.

23. Whitney-Brown, *Jean Vanier*, 54.

In light of these ideas, how might God's "mark" or God's image be understood in terms of the disabled? In fact, might the Church be able to assign meaning to the disabled in such a way that they are, in fact, valued just for who they are: persons created by the Spirit in the image of God? I would propose that Matthew's account of the Day of Judgment (Matt 25:31–46) gives an answer to the question of how the Church might define disabled persons' embodied self: they are the image of God in Jesus Christ.[24] "Jesus Christ the disabled God repudiates the conception of disability as a consequence of sin. Our bodies participate in the image of God, not in spite of our impairments and contingencies but *through* them."[25]

This view of God in Christ as "disabled" might mean that believers wrestle with perfectionist language and expectations of humans. Pentecostals have long identified with the holiness movement and its power and perfectionist emphases.[26] While certainly an important emphasis in regard to human sinfulness, the perfectionist emphasis and expectation have also been applied to those with disabilities. Cooper says that God in Christ seen in the poor, oppressed, and marginalized (and disabled) "reminds us to think of God's power christologically— God's being with us, suffering with us, broken for us."[27] This is possible only because Christians take seriously Paul's assertion that "nothing can separate us from the love of God in Christ Jesus" (Rom 8:38–39). The mystery of the affliction the disabled seem to bear would have some believe that the disabled are somehow far less than "perfect" and thus not loved by God. Perfectionism is not the issue here. The only expectation people in the faith community should have for any person, disabled or not, is that every person is loved—loved by God and loved by the faith community. With the apostle's confident assertion about the certainty of God's love, the mystery of the affliction of the disabled is at least partially explained: that God should be understood to be in the life of any person, disabled or not, can only be explained by God's love.[28]

---

24. Hare, *Matthew*, 290–91. Douglas Hare makes a good summary case for the person of Jesus to be seen in all the poor, oppressed, and marginalized of the world, not just those in the Church.

25. Eisland, "Encountering the Disabled God," 14; (emphasis in original).

26. See Hull, "Broken Body in a Broken World," 5ff.

27. Cooper, "Disabled God," 178.

28. Ibid., 180.

On the one hand, this approach to the work of the Spirit and the understanding of God's image in disabled persons can free the Church to view the disabled as persons of worth who reflect the image of Christ and who are the recipients of the love of God. On the other hand, the Church might view the disabled as those who virtuously endure affliction for the sake of Christ, as though the disability were a required "burden" for the disabled to bear to be considered "spiritual." Nancy Eisland has expressed well what this might mean for the disabled: "Disability is seen as a temporary affliction that must be endured to gain heavenly rewards . . . It has encouraged persons with disabilities to acquiesce to social barriers as a sign of obedience to God, and to internalize second-class status inside and outside the church."[29]

In addition to the Church's viewing of the disabled through the lens of Jesus Christ, might also the disabled view themselves in the same way? If the Church were to try to "say" to the disabled (and/or to their families) by preaching, architecture,[30] church programs, and individual concern that they are valued, loved, and thus accepted as they are, might then the disabled view themselves differently? They just might consider this a kind of "permission" to view themselves as persons of worth through Jesus Christ. In describing her permanently disabled condition, Betenbaugh came up with a beautiful description that came from her study of the gospel message. She decided that her condition was a "symbol [she] would present [to the church] of *an Easter life, an Easter faith, being lived in a Good Friday body.*"[31]

---

29. Eisland, "Encountering the Disabled God," 12.

30. See the booklet entitled, *That All May Worship*, Ginny Thornburgh.

31. Betenbaugh, "Disability," 208; (emphasis mine).

5

Forming a Community of the Spirit: Hospitality, Fellowship, and Nurture

Dear friends, let us love one another, for love comes from God. Everyone who loves has been born of God and knows God. Whoever does not love does not know God, because God is love (1 John 4:7–8).

"Community . . . cannot grow out of loneliness, but comes when the person who begins to recognize his or her belovedness greets the belovedness of the other. The God alive in me greets the God resident in you. When people can cease having to be for us everything, we can accept the fact they may still have a gift for us. They are partial reflections of the great love of God, but reflections nevertheless . . . We see him or her as a limited expression of an unlimited love.

To live and serve and worship with others thereby brings us to a place where we come together and remind each other by our mutual interdependence that we are not God, that we cannot meet our own needs, and that we cannot completely fulfill each other's needs. There is something wonderfully humbling and freeing about this. For we find a place where people give one another grace. That we are not God does not mean that we cannot mediate (if in a limited way) the unlimited love of God. Community is the place of joy and celebration where we are willing to say, 'Yes, we have begun to overcome in Christ.' Such is the victory of the Cross.

Gratitude springs from an insight, a recognition that something good has come from another person, that it is freely given to me, and meant as a favor. And at the moment this recognition dawns on me, gratitude spontaneously arises in my heart."[1]

AN INVITATION TO LOVING HOSPITALITY

So MANY BELIEVERS HAVE organized their lives in such a way that the busy activities of modern life have prevented them from fully

1. Nouwen, *Turn My Mourning into Dancing*, 83–84.

engaging their faith in ways that involve a faithful community. Often, a "fast food" approach to the faith has meant that believers quickly complete as many "vital" activities as possible during their busy week so that they might fit in all of them. Usually, this means that so many important things—family meals, times for reflection and prayer, meaningful time for building a strong faith community—get shortchanged in the midst of frantic and hectic schedules. If there are to be faith communities constructed around the offer of loving hospitality and acceptance of all people regardless of their social, economic, racial, or mental background, or their status, or abilities, then that effort takes careful and concerted effort. It will require significant amounts of time, time that modern Western believers might not be willing to give.

Hectic schedules have made so many modern believers exhausted and burned out from all they think they have to do just in the normal routines of their lives, not to mention the busy activities often planned by and through their local church. This has often led in turn to ministry burnout. It is also true that creating a loving and hospitable faith community can involve tedious yet necessary tasks: someone has to open the church on Sunday morning and start the air conditioning or heat; someone has to make sure repairs to the church building are made; someone has to deal with the confused and rebellious teens in middle school; someone has to attend to the elderly, the infirm, the troubled. A loving, nurturing community does not spring up to full possibility, maturity, and genuine welcome to all without people engaging in some hard, sometimes tedious, but always essential work. Most would rather leave the hard work to others, and some tasks seem so mundane and useless that one can get discouraged and want to give up.

A young monk once spent months at a monastery helping to weave a tapestry. One day, he rose from his bench in disgust: "I can't do this any longer," he exclaimed. "My directions make no sense. I have been working with a bright-yellow thread, and suddenly I'm to knot and cut it short for no reason. What a waste."

"My son," said an older monk, "you are not seeing the tapestry correctly. You are sitting at the back, working on only one spot." He led the younger monk to the front of the tapestry, hanging stretched in the large workroom, and the novice gasped. He had been weaving a beautiful picture—the three kings paying homage to the Christ child—his yellow thread was part of the gleaming halo around the baby's head. What had seemed wasteful and senseless was actually magnificent.

Creating community, any kind of community, is fraught with pitfalls—human pride, human indifference, "busyness," work and family overload, and resistance to the completion of the tedious and mundane. Any community-creating has to be intentional, arising from fervent prayer and trust that the Spirit will make possible for diverse people a community of truth, love, and learning despite human selfishness and personal agendas for success or happiness. Thus, any effort on the part of believers to create a loving community of hospitality will have to include a focused intentionality and energy on the part of all.[2] Otherwise, believers will just meet to be meeting, going through the motions and not really meaning it. Such an atmosphere of indifference and fiction would not be worth the time expended.

Some might argue that they already experience in their community an atmosphere of loving hospitality. Definitions of loving hospitality can be as broad and general as there are people. A woman gushed about how good the fellowship was in her community. The only trouble with that comment was that most people in the community who were acquainted with her knew her to speak only to her close friends and rarely, if ever, have much to do with others in the community. Yet she was completely sincere in her belief that the fellowship in the community was "great." It was clear that she was a very private person who preferred her fellowship only with those she chose; she did not comprehend that many had felt slighted by her failure to connect with them. She did not understand community or fellowship at all.

Others might argue that lively worship services are all that is necessary for creating community. If people worship together, the reasoning goes, the Spirit will strip away differences and draw people to Christ and to each other. This implied kind of "worship experience" often means very loud, raucous music led by a worship band for an extended period of time. This is followed by a long sermon or Bible teaching, often interspersed with videos or illustrated with power point slides. A few church leaders—the professional ministerial staff and talented voluntary worship band—dominate the entire worship time, providing no time or opportunities for diverse people to talk to each other, pray with each other, laugh or weep with each other. This is further complicated by so many who are already stressed and busy and just don't want to be bothered

2. Gibbs, *ChurchNext*. Hospitality is one of the empirical indicators of a missional church according to Eddie Gibbs.

with anything more than lively worship and a good sermon and a quick exit from the church parking lot.

Yet another complication in community-building is the Western notion of individualism and individual rights, especially the "right to privacy." A strength of this cultural attitude has been the production of great accomplishments by gifted individuals; this cultural emphasis creates an atmosphere in which anyone who has the right amount of ambition can achieve great things with minimal governmental or cultural interference. A weakness of this cultural attitude has been the creation of selfish, self-serving people who can be contemptuous of those who are different or considered less motivated than they. If people insist on their "right to privacy" as some kind of mysterious "divine right" of their faith over their commitment to Christ and His body, community-creating can be hampered if not destroyed. A believing community cannot be a place of loving hospitality if believers prefer privacy and are driven by ambition. In spite of this common insistence upon personal rights and privacy, loneliness seems to prevail in Western society.[3] Practicing loving hospitality may very well mean giving up significant "privacy" as we "carry each other's burdens, and in this way . . . fulfill the law of Christ" (Gal 6:2).

Settings traditionally available for community-building to occur have become rare. The Sunday school in many churches has almost disappeared. Bible studies in homes or home fellowship groups have disbanded. Specialty groups—youth, the elderly, men, women—still exist, but often are organized in the same way that church worship services are organized (structured to the extent that all but eliminates open interaction between congregants). It is hard to create community when the same kinds of things are being done in different settings. Each church can recognize that clear definitions of community and fellowship are needed, as well as settings where true community, true fellowship can occur. These settings can be as diverse as the local churches where they might occur.

Regardless of the setting or opportunity for community-creating and fellowship-forming, the process can begin with *loving hospitality*. Letty M. Russell has given a good definition of hospitality: "The practice of God's welcome embodied in our actions as we reach across differences to participate with God in bringing justice and healing to our world in

---

3. Jones, "You're Lonely, I'm Lonely," 35. He cites a recent study of loneliness in which it is described as contagious.

crisis."[4] Using the Tower of Babel and Day of Pentecost stories, she calls for people of faith to practice openness and kindness to all, regardless of differences. "When reading the story of Babel in conjunction with Acts 2, we see that unity comes, not through building a tower of domination or uniformity, but through communication."[5] It is in Christ, she argues, that "unity is the impossible possibility" so that "each of us will cease to live *apart* from one another and become *a part* of God's beautifully diverse creation."[6]

Russell attempts to do what she calls "re-frame" a theology of justice "in terms of social structures of justice and of partnership across barriers of difference."[7] Using the biblical stories of cities of refuge, she recommends the creation of "safe space" wherein the well being of all of creation is given great attention. To illustrate her ideas, she gives an extended interpretation of the story of Ruth, which she hopes "might be viewed as a metaphor of God's New Creation where all are partners with each other and God through our acts of hospitality."[8] Russell also uses the prophet Amos to insist on the practice of justice in the expression of hospitality (cf. Amos 5:24). "God's welcome is then an act of both love and justice through the offer of unbounded hospitality."[9] As people practice "mutual welcome," they might be surprised by the divine presence "unawares."[10]

Many believers might argue that a hearty welcome is provided all visitors to the local church, and these believers might sincerely believe they are doing all they can to provide loving hospitality. However, sometimes the views of visitors might be different from the perceptions of the regular attendees. Is there only a cursory welcome provided? Is it clear to the visitors that only certain kinds of people are truly welcome while others are just formally recognized? Is there expressed a kind of paternalism in the welcome offered (i.e., is the hospitality offered only from a dominant position)? If genuine hospitality exists in a community its effects will be evident. Henri Nouwen describes some of these effects:

4. Russell, *Just Hospitality*, 2.

5. Ibid., 59.

6. Ibid., 68; (emphasis in original).

7. Ibid., 82.

8. Ibid., 96.

9. Ibid., 107.

10. Ibid., 82–83.

Hospitality makes anxious disciples into powerful witnesses, makes suspicious owners into generous givers, and makes closed-minded sectarians into interested recipients of new ideas and insights.[11]

Like Russell, Yong also emphasizes God's expression or extension of hospitality to all through those who belong to God's kingdom, but Yong also emphasizes Jesus as an exemplary *recipient* of hospitality, from his birth in an offered stable to his burial in an offered tomb. Yong uses the phrase "free space" and says this is created by hospitality and describes it this way:

> Christians must discern the Spirit's presence and "perform" appropriate practices in concert with the hospitable God. They must embody Christ's incarnational vulnerability and open up theological and relational "free space" not only to serve as hosts for the gospel but also risk being guests of others.[12]

In extending loving hospitality, believers might create a "free space" (Yong) or "safe space" (Russell) in their local faith communities where believers can both extend and receive expressions of hospitality among those who attend as God's representatives, and thus in the process, begin to create a community of truth, justice, and love. This will require humility and vulnerability toward those who are welcomed into the community. Do we have the humility to welcome "strangers" with the possibility that we might be "entertaining angels" (Heb 13:2)? Do we recognize Christ in those who are different, hurting, or strange (Matt 25:31ff.)? It cannot be emphasized too much to say that *both the expression and reception of loving hospitality is the only way true community can even begin to be possible.*

In his short story, "The Three Hermits," Leo Tolstoy tells about a bishop on a pilgrimage on a ship with other pilgrims.[13] At one of the ports where they docked on their journey, the bishop overheard some sailors describing three hermits who lived on a deserted island nearby and who were trying to live for God. When the bishop heard this he insisted that the sailors take him there so the bishop could meet them and teach them a little about the faith. When he arrived on the island, the hermits warmly greeted the bishop. They told him of their simple lives of faith and service to each other and recited their simple prayer for the bishop.

---

11. Nouwen, *Wounded Healer*, 89.

12. Yong, *Hospitality and the Other*, 132.

13. Tolstoy, *Walk in the Light*, 253–60.

The bishop insisted on teaching them more about the faith and also required them to learn the Lord's Prayer. All day he tried reciting it to them and having them say it back. It was a difficult chore, for all three hermits were uneducated men. Finally, at the end of the day, the bishop thought they had learned to pray and had learned the rudiments of the faith. The sailors then took him back to his ship.

Late that night sailors on the ship in which the bishop and pilgrims were traveling awoke the bishop to tell him of a strange light approaching the ship. The bishop and the pilgrims gathered to watch the light. As it approached it became clear that the light was illuminating the three hermits walking on the water toward the boat. All on the ship were astounded. When they arrived, they shouted to the bishop to teach them again the Lord's Prayer for they had forgotten it after he had left. Here is what the bishop said: "Your own prayer will reach the Lord, men of God. It is not for me to teach you. Pray for us sinners." And the bishop bowed low before the old men; and they turned and went back across the sea.[14]

SPIRIT-ENABLED FELLOWSHIP

Gordon Atkinson described his first experience of a Quaker meeting in which worship consisted of sixty minutes of silence, interrupted only by different ones who would rise to speak briefly. He first experienced anxiety when someone would speak, but noticed the Quakers gave each person their attention until he or she was finished; then they would return to thoughtful meditation. He decided at the second meeting he attended that he could relax and participate in the silence and sense of community.

> When someone speaks at a Quaker meeting, that person has no power to change the meeting or the rules or the nature of the community. If the gathered people sense the presence of the Spirit in the speaker's words, there are tried and ancient methods for testing that. But no one feels threatened. Everyone is free to put his or her energy into hearing the person. Quakers are accustomed to seeking the wisdom of God in the words of a brother or sister.[15]

Such thoughtful and careful attention to each other as all have a chance to speak or participate is at the very heart of Spirit-enabled fellowship.

14. Ibid., 260.

15. Atkinson, "Listening Place," 12–13.

Testimony time has traditionally been a distinctive of Pentecostal worship. People have been given a chance in worship to share prayer requests, answered prayers, deep hurts and longings, concern for loved ones. During this time in worship the operation of the spiritual gifts would sometimes occur and many would be blessed. All might feel a particular closeness after the experience. Mark J. Cartledge calls testimony ". . . the integrating center of Pentecostal and charismatic epistemology."[16]

It is through finding a connection with both the biblical story and personal stories of faith that members of a believing community become connected with one another. Hearing members relate their experiences with the biblical stories and their own encounters with God can help others in the community to find their own connections with both the Bible and the Spirit. Knowing the stories creates a bond of fellowship with God and with others enabled by the Spirit. Even mainline churches seem to be recognizing the value of testimony.[17]

In his commentary on 1 and 2 Samuel, Walter Brueggemann notes the power of speech in the stories in the Samuel narratives:

> People talk to one another, and their talking matters. The playful possibility of speech is at work in the public process of Israel. People listen and are changed by such speech, and God is drawn deeply into the conversation. That is how Israel discerns what has happened in its memory and in its life.[18]

Pentecostal people can learn to talk to each other, to discern the Spirit's voice in each other's stories. They can also learn to appreciate the power of the story to make a difference in their lives.

The Bible is a collection of *stories*—testimonies—about God's saving deeds. It is God's intention that "God's name might be proclaimed in all the earth" (Exod 9:16) by God's people through testimony. God's name is best proclaimed in telling the stories of God's saving deeds in human history (Ps 78:1–8ff.). The ultimate divine saving deed is that of Jesus Christ as expressed in the gospel story. It is in that story—THE story—that believers can find a reference point for their little lives—THE story becomes MY story. Here is how Jurgen Moltmann put it:

---

16. See Cartledge, *Practical Theology*, 52–62.

17. Daniel, *Tell It Like It Is*; and Long, *Testimony*.

18. Brueggemann, *First and Second Samuel*, 5.

> The proclamation of the gospel always belongs within a community, for every language lives in a community or creates one . . . The fellowship which corresponds to the gospel in its original interpretation is the messianic community . . . It is a "story-telling fellowship," which continually wins its own freedom from the stories and myths of the society in which it lives, from the present realization of this story of Christ.[19]

Many works have been published proving that humans learn in the form of stories. In one such work, the writer makes the point that people understand life events only as they are able to attach those events to a story. He claims that it is the only way people make sense of their world.[20] Since a well-told story is powerful and influential, biblical writers used stories to persuade God's people to be faithful and to obey God. Stories of God's saving deeds in times of distress for the faith community became important for the faithful person to hear. Hearing these stories made it possible for individual believers to place their lives in God's hands.[21]

I like to think of our hearing the biblical story as a kind of "intersection" of believers' stories with *the* story. By making the biblical story the reference point for my little story I discover where I fit in God's story. My behavior, character, and destiny are altered. By making the biblical story the filter for my little life's story I remain accountable and responsible. Like a foundation for the building that is my life, the biblical story keeps me truly "grounded" and safe when the winds of the world, the flesh, and the devil blow my way. The more distance created from the biblical story, the more likely believers will succumb to those winds and face ultimate collapse. The tighter believers remain connected to the biblical story— their foundation—the greater will be their confidence and security that is found only in an obedient relationship with the Creator as expressed by the biblical story.

Regardless of the profession to which believers are called, knowing the biblical story is important. Business people will work for a company or a corporation that has a story. Pastors called to minister at a church learn that each local church has a story. Teachers in the public schools learn that every child has a story and that a story comes out of that community where their students live. Psychologists will hear others' stories,

19. Moltmann, *Church in the Power of the Spirit*, 225.

20. F. Smith, *To Think*, 63–64.

21. Amit, *Reading Biblical Narratives*, 2.

many of which they will be asked to interpret. Whatever laypeople are called to do and wherever they go they will be asked to hear stories and often interpret them, sometimes for others, always for themselves.

It is in the hearing and interpreting of stories that believers can find the intersection points with the biblical story. Thus, hearing the biblical story can be exciting and rewarding; it need not be boring and exhausting. Not only can laypeople hear and analyze the biblical story, they can also learn to tell their story better in relation to *the* story. And, with others in mind, lay believers can begin to think creatively about how they can help others intersect with the biblical story. I want to try to find ways my life's story intersects with the biblical story. And what a difference it makes!

Having discovered great truths within the biblical story, laypeople can then tell the story, and, by telling the story, communicate those truths. When Jesus wanted to speak of the risky, scandalous, and longsuffering love of God for God's people, he told a story about two sons, one who asked for his inheritance so he could do as he pleased and another son who had no pity or mercy for the other, caring only for himself. For centuries believers have called this story the story of the prodigal son (Luke 15:11ff.), and it communicates great theological truths in story form.

When God wanted to call Israel back to God from their idolatry, God sent the prophet Hosea to the nation. Through his painful experience with his wife, Hosea was able to communicate both his story and the story of God's saving mercy and love to an idolatrous people. Imbedded within the story of Hosea and Gomer is a bigger story of God's longsuffering love for God's people. When God wanted to tell the people God was willing to reshape them according to the divine plan, God sent Jeremiah to the potter's house (Jer 18:1–12). There, Jeremiah understood the story within the story. God was like the potter Jeremiah saw, who was willing to work with marred pieces (people) to reshape them into vessels useful and worthy to God. The story told the people of God's concern for them and of God's sovereign control over the clay (the people).

We can see in these stories certain transactions occurring that draw people into the story-world created by the biblical narrator. The story-world created invites the hearer/reader to live in a world where all sorts of transactions are possible. The story is presented in such a way that though times, places, traditions, and even events may change, the story-world is not finally bound by these changes. The story contains inexplicable, divinely enabled elements that make possible future transactions for people willing to enter this world and hear and see with the ears and eyes of faith. This makes it possible for people of faith to live obediently according to the transactions of the narrative. Jeremiah spoke of a "Potter-God" who was willing to reshape sinful people. Is the Potter-God still willing to reshape sinful people and make them obedient children of God? The answer is a resounding, "Yes!" The task will be to discover how believers can retell those stories in a form that is understandable to those in our cultures.

What might help to make hearing the biblical story so powerful is hearing the stories of others in which they describe how they wrestled with important life issues and with their faith. Through hearing these stories, believers become connected to each other in ways that are impossible except by this method. Testimony time in Pentecostal worship is only the beginning, albeit an important beginning. It is in testimony time that believers learn more about each other. Conversations of depth and meaning can continue long after worship time is over when believers learn more about the stories of brothers and sisters. Using examples from the Psalter in which psalmists describe their experiences with Torah and with God, Scott Ellington asserts that this process of testimony "is essential because it legitimates the community's stories and allows for their re-appropriation."[22] He described it this way:

> Truth-as-testimony offers a promising way in which to understand the Bible's truth-claims. Testimony involves selective remembering and includes the beliefs of the one testifying, along with references to the events that are believed to be true. Furthermore, it is at times possible to evaluate testimony about God through the continuing process of bringing together that testimony and fresh experiences of God's presence and absence. The common thread that allows the bringing together of the worldview(s) of the biblical writers and the worldview(s) of Pentecostals is a commonly held belief that God remains an active agent (indeed the primary active agent) in the biblical stories.[23]

What may seem strange to some is this connection of testimony and fellowship. It is important to understand just how vital it is for be-

22. Ellington, "History, Story, and Testimony," 260.

23. Ibid., 262; (parentheses in original).

lievers to intertwine their lives in the faith community. The best way to do that is to hear each other's stories. As believers become familiar with their brothers and sisters in Christ, they learn about each other's hurts, concerns, joys, and anxieties. They learn about their loved ones, their work, their neighborhoods. In brief, they become connected through the telling of their stories.

Miroslav Volf has made the point well about relationships within the believing community. He has noted that new believers do not attain full maturity in Christ when they come to faith in Jesus Christ. It is through fellowship with others that believers can grow to maturity. Volf observes,

> Just as a person cannot arise, develop, and live apart from her relationships with others, neither can a Christian exist as a Christian before entering into relation with other Christians; she is first constituted as a Christian *through* these relations.[24]

It is through testimony, conversation, education, nurture, and worship that believers are brought to maturity and maintained in their faith as God's grace works by means of God's spirit in and through the community. C. Ellis Nelson put it well when he said that a Christian faith matures,

> . . . when life experiences are interpreted in the light of the Christian tradition in order to understand and do the will of God amid ongoing events in which that person is involved. Because a congregation is part of the Body of Christ, it is the place where individuals receive guidance, as they work out the meaning of their experiences, and (find) support as they attempt to follow the leading of God's Spirit.[25]

As a young, zealous convert to Christ at age eighteen, I was anxious to share my faith with others in my small hometown in western Oklahoma. I measured spirituality by vocal, energetic expressions of the gospel. I was convinced that others weren't in what I deemed at the time to be spiritual groups and that the groups they were in were "less spiritual" than my group. It was not long before I learned a hard lesson from one of those so-called "less spiritual" people. A humble man who owned a drugstore in my small hometown was known for his kindness

24. Volf, *After Our Likeness*, 178; (emphasis in original).

25. Nelson, *How Faith Matures*, 18.

and regular church attendance, but not much else. Imagine my surprise when, in one of my forays into personal evangelism in the community, I discovered that for months the druggist had gone to a very poor man's home to give pain shots twice a day to a destitute man with terminal cancer whom the poor man had taken in. He gave these shots despite the fact that he had a business to run and a family to care for. And he did so without fanfare or recognition.

The druggist's witness showed me that a true witness provides more than just a tract and a gospel sermon; a true witness also is *there* to offer comfort and loving assistance to those who are hurting and needy. The destitute man did not need a gospel tract or a sermon; he needed a humble servant who would demonstrate true concern by giving him every day the medicine he needed in order to live. I was *telling* the poor man and his friend how to be a follower of Jesus Christ; the pharmacist was *showing* him how to be a follower of Christ. That "sermon" by the pharmacist was better than any I would preach!

Fellowship of the Spirit (*koinonia*) was a key characteristic of the Early Church after the outpouring of the Spirit at Pentecost (Acts 2:42). As a part of this Spirit-enabled fellowship, believers shared their worldly goods with each other, met regularly, and had meals together (Acts 2:44–46). These are all important activities for creating strong connections, relationships of meaning and depth. Perhaps *koinonia* might be better translated "to share in" or "to be involved in partnership with one another"[26] through various kinds of community activities. These fellowship activities also resulted in others joining their community as new believers (Acts 2:47). Spirit-enabled fellowship resulted in a kind of successful community evangelism. Volf noted the evangelistic dynamic of fellowship:

> The church is the fellowship of siblings who are friends, and the fellowship of friends who are siblings. Of course, these two metaphors describe the relationships within the interior ecclesial sphere and suggest that the church is an intimate group. Other metaphors must complement these to make it clear that the church is an "open" fellowship of friends and siblings who are called to summon enemies and strangers to become friends and children of God and to accept them as friends and siblings. Only such open fellowship is commensurate with the ultimate vision of the church as the eschatological gathering of the entire people of God from all tribes and nations.[27]

26. Leonard, "Church and the Laity," 625.

27. Volf, *After Our Likeness*, 181.

It is important to remember 1 Corinthians and the various difficulties in the Corinthian church that Paul addressed. The believers could hardly experience Spirit-enabled fellowship with one another when they had broken into factions: I follow Paul; I follow Apollos; I follow Peter; I follow Christ (1 Cor 1:10–12). They could hardly share Spirit-enabled fellowship when some still ate food offered to idols (1 Cor 10:14–22) and others were preoccupied with charismatic gifts without love (1 Cor 14:18–20). Instead of loving and supporting one another through Spirit-enabled fellowship, wealthy believers had shut out fellow believers who were marginalized by that society because of their poverty. In fact, in all of the problems Paul mentioned in 1 Corinthians, divisions created in the community have resulted in hardship and dissension rather than peace and a sense of community. Paul rightfully claimed that such an atmosphere is not in keeping with the work of the spirit of God.

Early Christians often took a meal together called the Love Feast. This feast involved people bringing what they could to eat (potluck!) to be shared with the community. William Barclay pointed out that this was practiced during the main meal of the day when all were supposed to eat slowly and enjoy each other's company.[28] As a part of that Love Feast, the faith community would also have partaken of the Lord's Supper. However, instead of being a time when all are nourished by both the meal and the remembrance of Christ's death, the Corinthian believers made their gatherings occasions when some were humiliated (1 Cor 11:21–22).

The humiliation involved the wealthier people (in whose homes such meals would have been provided since these homes were large enough to accommodate the believers) who were eating the best food and wine and leaving little or no food or drink for their poorer brethren. In first-century Greek homes there was a special dining room for honored (and presumably wealthy) guests to sit and eat. Lesser (and presumably poorer) guests would have been asked to stand in the larger room adjoining the dining room.[29] In other words, the wealthy Corinthian believers were observing social or status distinctions in clear violation of the spirit of the gospel—all were to share equally of the provisions of the community. How disgraceful, then, for the rich Corinthian believers to be eating and drinking to excess while their poorer brethren go without! What kind of gospel witness was that?

28. Barclay, *Letters to the Corinthians*, 102.

29. Hays, *First Corinthians*, 196. Richard Hays points out numbers of ancient Greek texts testifying to this division of guests in Greek homes.

An interesting wordplay is found in Paul's use of the Greek verb, *synerchesthai*, "to come together" (1 Cor 11:17,18, 20, 33, 34). When they "come together" they do not "come together." It means that when they come together for worship and fellowship they are not united in their witness to the gospel. They try to maintain social status rather than try to remove all class distinctions and freely share what they have with one another. This division is damaging to everyone. The problem here is not in the way they performed the ritual of the Lord's Supper; it is that they do not recognize the Body of Christ, the people of the faith community (1 Cor 11:29). Already, Paul hints of judgment in verse 19. Paul noted a certain difference as necessary for a distinction to be made; however, the difference Paul had in mind was not the difference between rich and poor (social status), but between those who were "approved by God" (*dokimoi*) and those who were not! In other words, what brought God's judgment in the Lord's Supper were actions that caused harm to one another. As Barclay put it, "A church is no true church if the art of sharing is forgotten."[30]

In essence, this description of the divisions within the Corinthian church is a kind of testimony, too. Their testimony (by their behavior) was not one of Spirit-enabled fellowship but one of division and class distinction. In such an atmosphere, poor believers' stories were silenced. The wealthy believers were not listening.

If there is to be Spirit-enabled fellowship through testimony—interacting with the biblical story and believers' life stories—more than a speaker is required. Also required are people who are willing to listen to what the Spirit might be saying and willing to listen to what fellow believers are trying to say—sometimes the Spirit is speaking through what fellow believers are trying to say. Brueggemann has eloquently expressed the importance of listening:

> We are created for listening. It is our proper business. We are made for communion, but the communion for which we are formed is not that of mindless camaraderie. It is a communion with the One who has hoped us and made us and summoned us and who waits for us . . . Our life consists in coming to terms with that One. We yearn to come to terms by listening. In the Bible, obedience takes the form of listening. The obedient life is one in which Israel listens, attends to, and responds to the voice of God . . . Listening of any se-

30. Barclay, *Letters to the Corinthians*, 102.

rious kind is difficult. Listening is more difficult if the substance is [God's] command, for such listening is the end of our self-control and our self-sufficiency. We are schooled in self-control and self-sufficiency and now God's powerful voice of command sounds, which destabilizes our favorite posture in the world. Listening is difficult for us because the modern world is organized against serious speech, against authoritative speech, against listening, against passionate discourse that binds one to another and causes one to yield to another. The notions of self-sufficiency and autonomy that govern our consciousness make listening difficult and obedience nearly impossible.[31]

It is possible for God's powerful voice to speak clearly through the testimonies of all believers. As the Body of Christ, believers need one another in many ways, but perhaps need each other most fundamentally by their careful attention to each other. By attentive listening to the testimonies of fellow Christians, all believers just might hear the voice of the Spirit. They might hear of ways they can be helped, or they might hear of ways they can help others.

Careful attention to people who are telling their stories—testifying—creates a true bond of respect and integrity. There is great power in hearing and being heard, but that can come only in a community where all are given a chance to speak and where all testimony is taken very seriously.

In the faith community it is also possible to have "voices" that are unable to speak. Those whose disabilities or social awkwardness might prevent their voices from being heard in testimony may be encouraged to find other ways to testify. Some may express themselves through drama, music, or just their personality; others "testify" by their kind and caring attitude, thus conveying their intrinsic value to the Body of Christ. Those who cannot speak may require other believers to be their voice so that their "testimony" is also included in the community's story.

My son is afflicted on the severe side of the autism spectrum. He is nonverbal and profoundly mentally handicapped. However, when he was twenty, his teacher in his special education class wrote a note to us one day that read:

> I wanted you to know how wonderful your son is. Today I had some bad news and I was crying. I went into the bathroom to wipe my tears and Phillip came to the door and said, "You okay?" He was the only one to take notice and I truly appreciate that!

31. Brueggemann, *Finally Comes the Poet*, 81–82.

Who will verbalize such testimonies in church? Here is a nonverbal person who somehow found just enough of a voice to express his concern to a hurting person. It is both a miracle that he spoke spontaneously and appropriately and that his simple speech was directed to assisting someone in need. How many stories or testimonies like this from nonverbal people remain untold?

At this point in this narrative, it is certain that most believers would give enthusiastic assent to what has been written: a faith community can provide a place of hospitality for all, encourage the formation of a listening community, and hear the biblical stories and the testimonies of the gathered saints, even those who are inarticulate and require help from the believing community. If only this did not sound so idealistic, as though it were an egalitarian dream. What about all the messiness, fleshliness, and foolishness found in even the best of faith communities?

Those who have participated in Pentecostal church services in which testimony was encouraged will, no doubt, recall painful moments when people decided to use the time for lengthy speeches of complaint, or rambling accounts of who-knows-what, or the same old line about gratitude for salvation, sanctification, and Spirit-baptism. Many would cringe when certain ones would stand to testify, certain that they were about to unleash something strange or lengthy with little connection to the work or voice of the Spirit.

The result of this kind of frustrating experience with testimony time has been its gradual disappearance from the Pentecostal church. This seemed to have started with attempts by professional ministers to control the content of testimonies. In 1989, Margaret Poloma reported,

> In many large churches testimonials have become professionalized. Selecting persons to give testimonies may eliminate the potential problems of the practice but at the expense of charismatic spontaneity. When eliciting a testimony from someone in the congregation, some pastors use the "question-answer" format of television talk shows, for it gives the pastor control over what is shared.[32]

---

32. Poloma, *Assemblies of God at the Crossroads*, 202–3. At the time of this publication, Poloma seemed certain that testimonials in church services would continue in the future (p. 203). Her prediction appears to have been premature, given anecdotal evidence of the disappearance of testimony time in AG churches reported to me from students through the years who have come to Southeastern University where I teach.

Certainly, it takes courage by church leaders to make sure there is order in all parts of church worship (or in whatever setting) according to the apostle's instruction in 1 Corinthians 14:26–33. However, the deletion of testimony time or the strict control of it by professional ministers actually robs the faith community of the powerful work of the Spirit in creating Spirit-enabled fellowship as well as ways the voice of the Spirit might be heard.

In subtle and not-so-subtle ways, the message by church leaders to the congregation might be that lay voices in testimony are not welcomed and will not be heard. An unspoken yet very clear message might be conveyed that only the pastoral staff and the worship team are allowed to express themselves publicly in church meetings. As a result, laypeople learn that silence is valued and that listening is a one-way street—the pastoral staff and worship team may speak, the laypeople must listen.

It is in community worship or settings in which all voices can be heard—Sunday school class, home Bible studies, prayer meetings—that Pentecostal people have claimed, "the Spirit is in control." If that is the case, more people than the pastoral staff and worship team would have an opportunity to speak, share a hymn, or give a word "for the strengthening of the church" (1 Cor 14:26). This means that careful and active listening must be practiced by church leaders, both to give the "amen" to that which is confirmed as coming from the Spirit, and to give proper, gentle discipline to those who are "out of order" in that they are not speaking by the Spirit.

In my own early days of Pentecostal experience, I understood that worship was led by the pastor and church leaders, but there were at least two times during worship services when lay voices must be heard because these voices just might be speaking by the Spirit: (1) during testimony time and (2) during times at the end of the service when people gathered around the altar benches to pray. The only "control" exercised by the pastor might have been to encourage a person who had spoken too long to get to the point, or to stop someone from interrupting someone else.

In addressing the issue of the messiness and potential strangeness of testimonies during testimony time in worship, it is important to stress the work of discipleship. Disciples are ones who can learn from their mentors in all aspects of the faith, including how to testify. They learn how to listen to God as well as how to express what they think the Spirit is asking them to say or do. They can also learn to alter their explanatory style, (i.e., learn how to say what they feel compelled to say in words or song or prophecy appropriate to the setting).[33] Where else might they learn the appropriate language to express their story?

This is not to suggest that helping believers find the language to express their story means telling them what to say or trying to control what they say. It is good for believers to find the language by which they might testify to God's presence or absence, to their joys and sorrows; however, there will always remain an element of messiness, of untidiness. Believers can and will make mistakes in telling their stories, but a loving, nurturing community will be able to bear these mistakes as long as those testifying are trying to be authentic and faithful to God and their brothers and sisters.

In the faith, no one springs spontaneously to full blown maturity. All will make mistakes, but in a loving community where it is understood that all make mistakes, believers can find "permission" and encouragement to correct them. The potential for messiness or strangeness of testimony in testimony time during worship is not a satisfactory excuse for deleting it from community activities. Testimony remains a key method by which Spirit-enabled fellowship functions—believers need to express how God is working in their lives; other believers need to listen attentively for the voice of the Spirit.

It is also important to note that yet another weakness of testimony is the constant pressure always to have a good ending to one's story. Failure, lack of faith, and struggles may be told, but only in the context of eventual victory and success. If testimony represents an accurate description of believers' faith stories, then those stories are not always ones of success and "victory." Believers who suffer should not be chided for their unbelief or scolded into faith. Permission to lament must be granted. Condemnation of those who are hurting must itself be condemned. Instead of condemnation, other believers can offer their own "shoulder of faith" on which suffering believers, plagued by doubts, might lean for a season while they are seeking for equilibrium in their spiritual lives. Ellington has argued that "the loss of lament is related to an increasing loss of testimony in the praying community."[34]

33. Nerken, "Making It Safe to Grieve," 1093. While it is true that this article addresses grief, the principle of learning how best to express oneself applies here also. Believers can find the language of grief and the language of testimony with the help of a loving community.

34. Ellington, "Costly Loss of Testimony," 51.

If Spirit-enabled fellowship comes to fruition, it will come only as "truth-as-testimony"[35] (i.e., the testimony comes out as what is really going on in a person's life rather than only "acceptable" rhetoric related to success and "good" things). Without the possibility of transparency in testimony, the truth will usually be withheld. Often, a kind of fiction exists whereby is conveyed the idea that everyone is well and happy. Sadly, many who are unhappy are not allowed to say that. Believers thus do not know each other's full stories and cannot respond to others as the Spirit reveals. It is great to "rejoice with those who rejoice"; it is hard to "mourn with those who mourn" (Rom 12:15). Even if there are those who are suffering or are weak or failing, we can remember these words: "We who are strong ought to bear with the failings of the weak and not to please ourselves. Each of us should please his neighbor for his good, to build him up" (Rom 15:1–2).

The phrase, "to build him up," in the passage in Romans speaks to the therapeutic value in testimony. In seminary, I learned about pastoral counseling from Dr. John W. Drakeford. He believed that laypeople could be trusted to tell their stories to other believers to help them deal with the common problems that beset humans. He certainly believed in the work of professional therapists and psychiatrists for those clinically depressed; however, the majority of people simply need a caring community of believers willing to share their life stories in coping with the frustrations and hurts of everyday life. Dr. Drakeford called his method Integrity Therapy and advocated simple requirements of those practicing it: basic honesty, sensitivity to others, and a motivating concern for others.[36] The principles and techniques of his method are these: laity-led, high ethical standards, a concern for those in the group, an openness to confession of sins and hurts, restitution or putting things right and trying to heal any hurts, and a desire to take the message to others.[37] Through the practice of one believer telling another believer how she coped with a particular issue, the other believer might be able to learn how to cope with a similar issue. The power of such interactions came in the *integrity* of the experience related by someone in the group. In this way, the Spirit-enabled personal testimony to assist believers in handling life's difficulties.[38]

---

35. See Ellington, "History, Story, and Testimony," 260. The "truth-as-testimony" phrase from Ellington is used here to mean the whole truth of a person's spiritual life, not just the happy or "victorious" parts.

36. Drakeford, *Integrity Therapy*, 12.

37. Ibid., 52.

38. See also Polischuk, "Caring Church," 66–71, which appeared in *Enrichment*,

In the past, God's word has come through tablets of stone and handwriting on a wall and through the pages of Scripture. It has come through a flood and a rainbow, a burning bush and a whirling wind. Through the correction of the prophets and the curses of Shimei. His word has thundered from Sinai and whimpered from a manger. His word has come through a dream in the light and a vision in the day. Through the mouths of kings and the mouths of babes. Through the psalms of God's anointed and the poems of pagans. Through a star in the night and through angels in the field. Through a poor widow's offering, the picture of a good Samaritan, and the story of a prodigal son. His word was spoken through the law of Moses and afterward, more eloquently, through the life of Christ. We live by those words and on those words, not by bread alone but by every word that proceeds from the mouth of God. Some of those words are spoken at the most unexpected of places that if we're not expecting, we'll miss. Some of those words are spoken by the unlikeliest of people whom we will most likely dismiss if we don't receive them. And some of those words come in the most uncommon of ways that we will react against if we're not accustomed to the unaccustomed ways that God speaks. These words are the daily bread of the soul. We have the responsibility to handle them accurately. But we have a more important responsibility to handle them reverently, for they are words from the King. However they come, through whatever messenger they come, they are *His* words, and we should receive them as such.[39]

---

the quarterly journal for Assemblies of God ministers; and Clinebell, "Experiments in Training Laity for Ministry," 35–43. Although at first glance, Dr. Polischuk and Dr. Clinebell appear to be advocating the use of laity for pastoral care and counseling, they create so many requirements for this work that I would imagine a pastor would find the practical application of this nearly impossible. Yes, Dr. Polischuk does emphasize the reliance upon the Spirit and the practice of biblical counseling; however, he insists on using only mature believers who have the spiritual gifts of wisdom and knowledge, and he insists on close professional ministerial oversight as well as extensive training by pastoral staff. Dr. Clinebell's article describes lengthy training sessions complete with required verbatims. This depth of involvement would discourage both pastor and laypeople. If someone needed this level of trained counseling, he or she should see a licensed professional or one of the pastoral staff instead of "trained" laity. Dr. Drakeford's integrity therapy simply helps people connect with others empathetically by helping them tell their stories of life and faith experiences. This approach seems to trust the power of the story and the storyteller in helping people deal with the usual life issues. For all other people dealing with issues only a clinician or trained pastoral counselor could handle, there would be referral.

39. Gire, *Windows of the Soul*, 216–18; (emphasis in original).

FORMING A NURTURING COMMUNITY

A mother was preparing breakfast for her two sons, Kevin, age five, and Ryan, age three. The boys began to argue over who would get the first pancake. Their mother saw the opportunity for a moral lesson. "If Jesus were sitting here, he would say, 'Let my brother have the first pancake, I can wait.'" Kevin turned to his younger brother and said, "Ryan, you be Jesus!"

Some people can get so caught up in their own agendas and schedules that they forget that there are others around who might be hurting. Sadly, they often come across as too selfish to take time out to help those who are hurting because that might mean they would get off their strict daily schedules or they might have to hurt a bit with someone. After all, don't they have enough troubles of their own without having to take on those of others? Let someone else deal with those hurting people. I will deal with my own needs, thank you very much. Those other folks who are hurting can deal with their own hurts themselves, just as I do.

Other people simply find themselves stressed and in need of loving nurture to sustain their faith. They need the warm embrace of a loving and accepting community as they negotiate the difficulties of living in a fast-paced society that expects so much of them in terms of job success, family wholeness, and psychological health and well being without providing the necessary supports for these things to happen. They need warm and loving nurture themselves, which often means they are unable to extend the same to others. They do not mean to be selfish and self-absorbed; they are just needy and weary.

To speak of love and nurture without recognizing real human stresses and strains is to ignore a common ailment of a hectic modern society. People are not surprised to be treated shabbily by a store clerk or fellow driver on the roadways. Who has not complained about a bored teenager who checked or bagged the groceries or a surly auto service manager who was barely civil when servicing the car? In such an atmosphere people become defensive because of the meanness encountered. Believers try not to be apathetic or mean in return, but often the atmosphere gets the better of them. At least they try to conceal their feelings with the thought that no one cares anyway, and certainly they don't want to contribute with their own cruelty to the overall meanness already prevalent.

In addition, the notions of love and nurture have been cheapened by casual sex in television programs and in most movies. It is also common for television programs and movies to present a casual view of marriage and relationship commitments, as well as to present scenes of friends in deep conflict and division; often perpetrating great acts of cruelty upon each other. It does not help when most adult believers can tell tragic stories of churches split over some sort of un-Christian and inhumane treatment of a particular group of believers or the unjust treatment of a capable pastor.

It takes great care to speak of love and nurture to believers who might be a bit jaded by a society so casual about love and relationships. These adult believers may have become cynics about love and nurture from hearing it widely proclaimed in churches they have attended where only anger and division was experienced instead. Speaking of love and nurture is a delicate task because so many have been hurt in some way by counterfeits or by selfish people whose words of love belied their selfish actions.

To speak of love properly—without sounding insincere or weepy and sentimental—is a difficult task. Appeals could be made to the "love chapter" in 1 Corinthians 13 or to Shakespeare's famous sonnets or even to the best Hallmark greeting cards prepared for Valentine's Day. Reading about love and declaring that love is the foundation of the two most important commandments is one thing, actually practicing that love is quite another when people are involved. As the old joke goes, "I could love the whole world if it weren't for all the people in it!" This is why the word "nurture" has been chosen instead of love. Of course, nurture must have love as its foundation and focus, but only speaking of love is inadequate; love requires sacrificial action. The apostle put it this way, "Dear children, let us not love with words or tongue but with actions and in truth" (1 John 3:18). Tom Long has told this story, which illustrates the loving nurture proposed here.

> Several years ago I was at a church in Alabama, scheduled to preach in the morning service. A few minutes before the service, the pastor got up from his desk and beckoned me to follow. "Come here," he said, "There's something I want you to see." I followed him down the stairs and into the educational wing. We approached a Sunday school classroom, and the pastor pointed to the glass window set in the classroom door. "Look," he urged.

I peered through the glass into a kindergarten class full of activity. In one corner of the room, a teacher was reading a story to a group of children. In another corner, a teacher was assisting children in building something with blocks. In still another area, children were gathered around an adult with a guitar, learning a new song. In the middle of the room sat an elderly woman, calmly and slowly rocking in a rocking chair. Every now and then, a child would break away from a group and come to sit on her lap as she rocked. Occasionally, the woman in the rocker would say something to one of the teachers, and the adult would respond with a laugh and a nod of the head. The actual teaching was being done around the edges and in the corners, but this aged woman in the center was radiating grace around the room. "She used to be the only kindergarten teacher," the pastor informed me. "But now that she is late in her life, others do the teaching. But she still comes every Sunday morning to sit in the center of the room and provide a blessing."[40]

Believers might get a warm feeling about the children being nurtured by the elderly woman, but, if hard pressed, might be persuaded to admit that they, too, need the kind of loving nurture she was providing the children. Were the children there because of the other children, the activities, or because of the nurture they received from the woman? What radiates from the center of my faith community?

Surprisingly, love—the true kind of love, God's love—is not an easy or casual subject. The power of the gospel to bring genuine empathy and relief to the hurts of others seems so remote in a busy, agenda-oriented, success-guided world. Yes, the local church is supposed to be a repository of such nurture, but for people harried and wounded by a hostile world there is great hesitancy and doubt of the possibility of love and nurture. And when we have spent six days protecting ourselves from verbal and emotional assaults, it is hard on the seventh day to break with old habits and believe the promise of God's nurture or make an attempt to lend another such promised nurture. After all, won't the other be suspicious or expect payment in return? Truly loving someone with the kind of nurture intended by my emphasis in this chapter might mean believers become vulnerable, open, and even willing to help bear the pain of others. People are practiced in guarding their hearts because life often breaks open hearts. We don't want to open our hearts and listen

40. Long, "Preaching in the Middle of a Saintly Conversation," 20–21.

so that we do not run the risk of the hurts that can come in. Listening with our hearts can actually be risky because it means that we also might suffer with the sufferers.

> . . . a life formed by love for others inevitably leads to one's own suffering, and this is true in Jesus' life and in the history of God . . . Jesus on the cross is God . . . made weak and vulnerable to worldly powers because of the perfection of divine love.[41]

The poet Perry Tanksley put it this way in his poem, "My Unbroken Heart":

> Regardless of the cost I sought to avoid
> The tragic hurt of being annoyed
> With a broken heart from loving someone
> To discover too late my love unreturned.
> Alas, I discovered while living alone
> My heart, unbroken, had turned to stone[42]

A story is told about Nouwen (now deceased), a Catholic priest and brilliant psychologist and theologian at Yale and, later, Harvard, who suddenly resigned his prestigious position at Harvard to become Director of Daybreak, a ministry to the severely mentally and physically handicapped in Toronto.[43] There were those who believed he had thrown away a brilliant career at Harvard to do something so insignificant and meaningless in regard to his gifts and talents—moving backwards from the way of society's recommendations and expectations. But this was certainly not his attitude about his decision.[44] His reaction was to describe his resignation from Harvard and move to Daybreak as God's call.

> If handicapped people express love for you, then it comes from God. It's not because you accomplished anything. These broken, wounded, and completely unpretentious people forced me to let go of my relevant self—the self that can do things, show things, prove things, build things—and forced me to reclaim that unadorned self in which I am completely vulnerable, open to receive and give love regardless of any accomplishments.[45]

41. Cooper, "Disabled God," 176.

42. Tanksley, I Call You Friend, 11.

43. See chapter 4 under the subhead, "Creation and Imago Dei: Who or What are the 'Embodied' Made in God's Image?" where the text describes L'Arche communities begun by Jean Vanier. See also Whitney-Brown, Jean Vanier, 54.

44. Boers, "What Henri Nouwen Found at Daybreak," 31.

45. Ibid.

It is a Spirit-enabled community that practices the first of the fruit of the Spirit listed in Galatians 5:22: love. In such a community where love is practiced and people are nurtured in their faith, there has to be the realization that truly loving and nurturing others might usually mean that weak and sinful people are the ones most in dire need of loving nurture. We are reminded of what the apostle said: "Brothers, if someone is caught in a sin, you who are spiritual should restore him gently. But watch yourself, or you also may be tempted. Carry each other's burdens, and in this way you will fulfill the law of Christ" (Gal 6:1–2). No one has described more eloquently love's particularity implied by that passage than Martin Luther.

> If there is anything in us, it is not our own; it is a gift of God. But if it is a gift of God, then it is entirely a debt one owes to love, that is, to the Law of Christ. And if it is a debt owed to love, then I must serve others with it, not myself. Thus my learning is not my own; it belongs to the unlearned and is the debt I owe them. My chastity is not my own; it belongs to those who commit sins of the flesh, and I am obligated to serve them through it by offering it to God for them by sustaining and [forgiving] them, and thus with my respectability, veiling their shame before God and [people] . . . Thus my wisdom belongs to the foolish, my power to the oppressed. Thus my wealth belongs to the poor, my righteousness to the sinners . . . It is with all these qualities that we must stand before God and intervene on behalf of those who do not have them, as though clothed with someone else's garment . . . But even before [people] we must, with the same love, render them service against their detractors and those who are violent toward them; for this is what Christ did for us.[46]

There are no secret or mystical formulas by which a nurturing community might be formed. It will require humble people who truly value what a nurturing community can provide, and value it above all else. Such a loving, nurturing community should be the natural product of Spirit-enabled fellowship. If God's love is really true, believers cannot help but convey that love in authentic, tangible ways. "There is no wavering in God's intent to love us, no matter what . . . [and] when we love and live in a community where love counts, we are at once ourselves and like God."[47]

46. Luther, *Lectures on Galatians*, 393.
47. Cooper, "Disabled God," 173–74.

The only "secret" to be addressed here is the reality of human selfishness and self-absorption. Eugene Peterson says it is necessary for believers to "unself" themselves, moving from self to community.[48] Commenting on the self-absorption of the psalmist in Psalm 77:4–9, Peterson has said, "The self meditating on the self is in a room without air, without oxygen. Left there long enough, breathing its own gasses, it sickens."[49] People are, by nature, selfish beings who need gospel transformation so that they might become children of God who " . . . use whatever gift [they] have received to serve others, faithfully administering God's grace in its various forms" (1 Peter 4:10). It is a kind of spiritual discipline believers acquire to be able to do this: "Nobody should seek his own good, but the good of others" (1 Cor 10:24).

> A life of compassion must be nurtured. This can only be done in the midst of hurt and pain, where wisdom is inaccessible to self-pity. God does not answer our self-pitying request but our need for unselfing. He enters our lives and provides prophet and priest to lead us into and through the wilderness of temptation and trial. Only then can we learn the ways of providence and discover the means of grace—a long, difficult, mercy-marked, grace-guided forty years that represents the middle of the journey for persons who live by faith. It is a journey through which we learn personal morality and social responsibility. Salvation is put to the work of building community, engaging in worship, encountering evil.[50]

CONCLUDING REMARKS

Many believers would agree that their congregations should be more oriented to hospitality, fellowship, and loving nurture; however, just how these things are accomplished is the great mystery. I could outline some strategies by which such things might occur, but the reality is that no one congregation is the same and "cookie-cutter" approaches to ministry are usually not successful in every place.

To get believers to focus more on hospitality, fellowship, and loving nurture might mean extended prayer sessions, a call for fasting and prayer, a challenge to the congregation by both pastor and lay leaders to reorient their lives by these concerns, or all of the above. The whole

48. Peterson, *Where Your Treasure Is.*

49. Ibid., 103.

50. Ibid., 108. Peterson's summary comments on his study of Psalm 77:13–20.

church must ask itself, corporately and individually: What is the true focus of this congregation? What is the true focus of my life of faith?

The reality might be that many congregations just do not want change to occur; they are very comfortable with things just as they are, thank you very much. Angie Ward has written about this attitude which she discovered after she and her husband began their ministry right out of seminary at an older, established church.[51]

> While that church on the surface valued outreach, character, and innovation, the no-rocking ethos meant that its actual directive was "Don't offend anyone; don't take risks; and don't deal with hidden sin." It took more than three years for us to figure this out, by repeated trial and error, but also by looking at our church's history, the personalities of its leaders, and even the culture of our surrounding community.[52]

She learned that believers resisted change with great fervor. They had become comfortable in the way things were and did not want to take any risks, make any changes. What was Ward's advice about this?

> Culture takes a long time to create, and even longer to change. Melting the tip of the iceberg does not eliminate the ice below the waterline. But in any church, the first step toward creating a healthy culture is identifying the existing ethos, whether positive or negative.[53]

Naturally, "melting the iceberg" can be a strenuous and often painful process. People will cling desperately to their old ways because change can be frightening and require from believers more than they are ready to give. Indeed, Ward reported in her article that she and her husband were unable to make the needed changes in that church; however, in their next pastorate, they were able to recognize the unstated core values and begin right away to make important changes. Nevertheless, those changes came slowly.

> From spiritual growth to evangelism to giving to ministry, a church that was founded as a safe place for those wounded by religion became a place for long-time Christians to be comfortable and inactive. Changing that culture, of course, is an ongoing

---

51. Ward, "Discerning Your Church's Hidden Core Values."
52. Ibid., lines 30–34.
53. Ibid., lines 53–55.

process. Slowly, but surely, our church is beginning to reflect a renewed purpose of "Life-changing relationships with God, with each other, and with the world around us."[54]

If lay and professional church leaders would take my proposals for loving hospitality, Spirit-enabled fellowship, and a nurturing community seriously, they might have to consider first the hidden core values of the congregation as they try to "melt the iceberg" of resistance to change. The values I am proposing are most certainly worth the effort.

Such a faith community carefully formed with the values I am proposing just might provide the right environment for implementing successfully the mission of the local church as understood in the Pentecostal tradition: proclaiming the gospel to the local community. If effective gospel witness should occur and people were to respond to the gospel, it would be important to have a supportive community for new converts to the faith.

In concluding this chapter, I wish to emphasize just how important a solid, functioning, nurturing, loving community is. From such a loving and healthy environment, well-balanced and more mature believers will emerge to make significant impacts in their various workplaces in the local community. Like children reared in a loving and nurturing family who become well-adjusted and productive adults, believers in the local church—the family of God—can exemplify the love and nurture learned in their faith communities, becoming effective ministers for Christ in public schools, the business world, the factory, and government services.[55]

54. Ibid., lines 59–64.

55. See Banks, "Community as a Loving Family," 46–57.

6

The Church Needs Its Pastor

Until about a century ago, what pastors did between Sundays was a
piece with what they did on Sundays. The context changed: instead
of an assembled congregation, the pastor was with one other person
or with small gatherings of persons, or alone in study and prayer. The
manner changed: instead of proclamation, there was conversation.
But the work was the same: discovering the meaning of Scripture,
developing a life of prayer, guiding growth into maturity.

This is the pastoral work that is historically termed the cure of
souls. The primary sense of "cura" in Latin is "care," with under-
tones of "cure." The soul is the essence of the human personality.
The cure of souls then, is the Scripture-directed, prayer-shaped care
that is devoted to persons singly or in groups, in settings sacred and
profane. It is a determination to work at the center, to concentrate
on the essential.[1]

COMPLEMENTARY, NOT COMPETITIVE

IN DESCRIBING WHAT I believe is the call of laypeople, I want to emphasize the role of the pastor. When reading what I will say about the
ministry of the laity, some might get the impression that I do not think
pastors are necessary. On the contrary, what I propose concerning the
ministry of the laity includes the conviction that God-called, Spirit-led
pastors are vital and most necessary for the completion of my vision for
the laity. However, the way I understand the role and duties of a pastor
might seem different from the current norm.

Pastors can view laypeople as partners in ministry; they can be
complementary and not competitive. My concern has to do with the
current popular ways pastors are viewed: as CEO, coach, entertainer,

1. Peterson, *Contemplative Pastor*, 57.

entrepreneur, or therapist. Each of these descriptive words suggests, in our culture, emphases that might be popular but also might not be in keeping with the biblical mandate described in 1 Peter 5:2–3:

> Be shepherds of God's flock that is under your care, serving as overseers—not because you must, but because you are willing, as God wants you to be; not greedy for money, but eager to serve; not lording it over those entrusted to you, but being examples to the flock.

The word *shepherd* in this passage suggests that pastors are to demonstrate real concern for their "flock"—believers entrusted to their care—protecting them from harm and helping them find God's path of righteousness and peace. Sadly, a current model in vogue tells pastors to keep some distance from their flock, except for those who are rich enough to fund the ministries of the church. Yet the text in 1 Peter plainly states that they are not to be "greedy for money." Peterson speaks about this in reference to pastoral visitation:

> The secularization of pastoral visitation takes place when the pastor gives up the uncertain and somewhat modest work of being a companion to persons in pilgrimage and takes on the job of public relations agent for the congregation; the job then is to whip up flagging enthusiasm, raise money for the budget, promote new programs, and "get out the vote" on Sundays. Even when people sense the manipulative nature of such visitation, they don't seem to mind—they are so conditioned to being treated in such ways by advertisers, politicians, and salespeople that they apparently assume that it is the mark of any successful person and admire the energy of the pastor who does it.[2]

The word *shepherd* also suggests that pastors are to make sure the people are fed on God's Word and understand the work of the Spirit. Finally, the passage commands pastors to serve their "flock" humbly and sacrificially. In all of these ways they serve as examples of what true ministry is. Rather than to be understood as a business manager, entertainer, or entrepreneur, pastors can be viewed as spiritual mentors and shepherds who love their "flock" and are deeply involved in their lives—the lives of everyone, not just the wealthy.

Pastors are vital to the Spirit-enabled church that I envision. In my view of pastoral ministry, the true work of the pastor is found in spiri-

2. Peterson, *Five Smooth Stones for Pastoral Work*, 93.

tual formation, biblical preaching and teaching, Spirit-enabled fellow-ship, and intercessory prayer. If pastors practice these things, they will be deeply involved in the lives of their congregations in humble, loving relationships. They will also need to have "multiple kinds of intelligence, abstract and practical" as they provide much needed godly wisdom to laypeople who are also called to serve.[3]

Spiritual formation has to be more than just loud and long worship services. Pastors can carve out time to preach about studying God's Word carefully and hearing the voice of the Spirit. Laypeople need to understand the importance of finding time for daily devotions. Spiritual formation will include the interior work of the Spirit that involves sanctification, purga-tion, confession of sin, and repentance. One spiritual practice pastors can help believers to develop is what Parker Palmer calls "our own authentic selfhood."[4] As believers we learn to abandon the "false self" and "recover and reclaim the gift" of our birthright—our true self.[5] We can learn not to be driven by "oughts" but by finding how our true vocation can "join self and service."[6] Pastors have the joy of helping believers to find spiritual wholeness so that they might experience God's joy in fulfilling their call-ing to the places of great need to which they are sent.

Wise pastors understand that spiritual formation includes deal-ing with the pain of grief and suffering and with the temptations of the world, the flesh, and the devil. Believers have to find ways to carve out regular times for reflection and renewal in a society increasingly expect-ing people to maintain a frantic pace. In addition, how can one hear the voice of the Spirit when so much media is readily available and highly sophisticated? Is there a "word from God" for the local community? For the congregation? For one's workplace?

> The pastor . . . has the responsibility of insisting that [for exam-ple] the Exodus event continues to be a design for salvation to the person who does piecework in a factory, to the youth who pumps gasoline, to the woman in daily negotiation with the demands of diapers and career, to the man trying to achieve poise between ambition in his profession and sensitivity to his wife and children at home. Pastoral work is a commitment to the everyday: it is an

---

3. Dykstra, "Imagination and the Pastoral Life."

4. Palmer, "Now I Become Myself," line 93.

5. Ibid., line 33.

6. Ibid., line 95.

act of faith that the great truths of salvation are workable in the "ordinary universe."[7]

Biblical preaching and teaching are the ways God uses the pastor to speak prophetically (forth-telling) to God's people, helping them learn about serving God faithfully, loving their neighbors authentically, and reading their Bible accurately. In interpreting the Bible, pastors must wrestle with changing cultural, political, and ethical expectations. Pastors must decide how the Bible impacts their congregations in terms of social, economic, and political justice. Are there systems in place in society that must be resisted because of the harm generated by those systems? Are there systems in place that can be affirmed and supported? How does the Bible teach us to make decisions about these things?

However, please note that the mission of the church is not to get more and more people to come to hear the pastor talk.[8] The goal of good preaching and teaching is the enablement of believers to serve God in their own places of call, not to require them to appreciate and affirm only the pastor's call to preach. "Dynamic [pastoral] leadership does not think first of how to retain control but how to give away as much as possible."[9] In "open source" thinking, pastors can listen carefully to the ideas and goals of laypeople as they think about how the Spirit is leading them to express their callings.[10] One pastor has asked this provocative question, "What if we gave away some of our control, trusting God's people to develop their own vision and not just execute ours?"[11]

The pastor's preaching can take into account that laypeople will be sharing their faith with others in their workplaces and neighborhoods. How can pastors help laypeople to accept their "mantle" of spiritual leadership in regard to their neighborhoods and workplaces? How can pastors through their preaching give powerful affirmation of lay leadership in those settings?

While laypeople might not be called to preach, they are called to express clearly their faith and concern to those to whom they are called. How can pastors' preaching help the laypeople to find their voice, too? Perhaps pastoral preaching can be informed by the concerns and ques-

---

7. Peterson, *Five Smooth Stones for Pastoral Work*, 33.

8. M. Robinson and Dwight Smith, *Invading Secular Space*, 93.

9. Ibid., 153.

10. Kerr, "Open Source Activists."

11. Ibid., lines 147–49.

tions of the laity. Some pastors have open forums periodically with their congregations to hear their concerns and questions about the preaching. In giving laypeople a voice in these areas, the pastor might become a better preacher.

Gordon MacDonald has been a successful pastor for a long time. Early in his pastoral ministry he learned to listen carefully to the stories of his parishioners. He discovered that they did not view the life of the church and their faith in the same way that he did. He had met weekly for two years with a group of laymen before he began to hear what they really thought. He said to himself, "If I knew the story of every person in my church, how would my preaching change?"[12] Out of his experience in listening carefully to the stories of his parishioners, he came up with important questions that he asks himself about different age groups, from those in their teen years to those in their seventies.[13] The questions he poses are excellent conversation starters that pastors can have with their parishioners.

The laity also needs to learn how to develop genuine fellowship with other believers. It is the pastor who will lead the congregation in forming a *Spirit-enabled fellowship* of believers where testimonies are encouraged and truly heard. Love and nurture are indispensable in developing a mature and healthy congregation. Wise pastors understand that an atmosphere of coercion or hostility is unhealthy and destructive. They know that God's peace will rest in places where love and nurture really count; they will direct their preaching and their prayers in that direction.

In finding an atmosphere of loving welcome, believers can begin to feel comfortable with each other. As they begin to intertwine their lives through Spirit-enabled fellowship, they learn how to trust each other and pray fervently for one another. In such an atmosphere, they can assist each other in discovering their spiritual gifts to be practiced in the local church and the world. Pastors can help believers in this process to begin to recognize and name their gifts and callings. These gifts and callings can then be confirmed publicly in worship services. Here is what one study of healthy congregations discovered:

12. MacDonald, "Incarnate Preaching," lines 151–52.
13. Ibid., lines 102–10.

> . . . as pastors begin to visit their members in their workplaces, their preaching and teaching and their understanding of their members' lives are completely changed. Pastors discover that people are indeed being faithful in their workplaces, but that no one has helped them name their God-given gifts at work. People can speak about how God is at work in their congregation, but they cannot name how God is present in their workplace . . . [14]

While pastors are prevented from conducting professional ministry in most secular workplaces, they can still schedule periodic visits with laypeople in their workplaces. A pastor's visit will signal to the layperson that her place of God's call—her workplace—is a legitimate place of ministry concern. The pastor's visit will also show respect to her as a fellow minister, one who is engaged in her ministry setting. Finally, a pastor's visit need not be more than just a couple of minutes, scheduled ahead of time and intended to coordinate with the worker's break time so as not to violate workplace rules. A pastor might simply acknowledge her work and whisper a quiet prayer for her before leaving. While this pastoral visit might seem insignificant to some, it would send a powerful message to the worker: her pastor cares enough to visit, pray, and acknowledge her in her place of ministry. Who knows? The pastor just might also learn something there that might help in sermon preparation.

These things will require *godly wisdom*. I will speak more about wisdom in chapter 8. These things will also require *intercessory prayer*. It is good to know that pastors encourage people to share their needs and then provide adequate time for prayer in public worship. However, in my emphasis on the call and ministry of the laity, pastors will encourage the members of the laity to testify to their successes as well as struggles in their callings. As others in the congregation become aware of the struggles, they can be called on to pray for each other. Pastors can inspire others to engage in intercessory prayer in their preaching and by their example. A grateful congregation appreciates a pastor who, the members know, is regularly praying for them and teaching others the need to engage in intercessory prayer.

> By listening attentively to a person's dreams, desires, and longings, and by sharing passionately a person's struggles, painful frustrations, and difficulties, significance is given to them. The differences become thereby not neurotic annoyances but items in the experience of salvation. By immersing himself or herself

14. Fortin, "Centered Life Initiative," 366.

in the relational details of a people, the pastor makes an index of prayers for them . . . The actual details of intimate needs and relational realities become the stuff of prayer. Desires are shaped into adoration and difficulties are formed into petitions.[15]

It is important to recall what Jesus said about his own mission and that of his followers when he called them together and said,

You know that those who are regarded as rulers of the Gentiles lord it over them, and their high officials exercise authority over them. Not so with you. Instead, whoever wants to become great among you must be your servant, and whoever wants to be first must be slave of all. For even the Son of Man did not come to be served, but to serve, and to give his life as a ransom for many (Mark 10:42–45).

If pastors are called to serve others, as the Lord demonstrated, then "prayer . . . when it is real is always a sacramental reenactment of Gethsemane."[16] How can pastors become "fully present" to serve those to whom they have been called?

It is also important to remember the Apostle Paul's true concern for those to whom he had been called. He said that he had shared with the Thessalonians not only the gospel but also his own life (1 Thess 2:8). When he suffered and was comforted by God, he described the whole experience as one that would also benefit the Corinthians with comfort (2 Cor 1:3–7).

Douglas John Hall describes such service and such intercessory prayer that involves suffering, sacrifice, and pain this way:

God will not hear prayer that is painless, that causes no inconvenience to its authors, that involves no bodily contact. We are responsible for those for whom we pray. We respond to God for them and we become God's response to them. It is not a matter of turning the whole thing back to God . . . to pray is to announce to God and to one another our readiness to accept God's invitation to participate in the vicarious life of the Christ, to become in deed as well as in thought and word his Body, and to extend his priesthood in and for the world. It is an awesome thing, and not to be entered lightly.[17]

---

15. Peterson, *Five Smooth Stones for Pastoral Work*, 60.

16. Hall, *When You Pray*, 83.

17. Ibid., 85.

The former president of Columbia International University in Columbia, South Carolina, was Robertson McQuilkin. His wife Muriel was diagnosed with Alzheimer's disease at a relatively young age: her early fifties. Their story was carried in segments in *Christianity Today* because it was so remarkable.[18] For some time she was able to stay at home alone, even though she was confused. "Stay at home" may be misleading because she often wandered off, but not to just any place. She often went looking for her husband, whose office was about a mile away at the university.

One time a friend found her wandering toward the university and took her home before calling her husband. When her husband arrived at home the friend was crying because of Muriel's bloody feet, feet she had bloodied walking barefoot in the street over hot asphalt and garden mulch and trash to get to the one she loved. Through his tears the friend could only say, "Such love, such love." Even in her condition, she tried to keep doing what she had always done—to love and care for her husband. Loving and caring for her husband had been the habit of her life. Old habits die hard.

McQuilkin was so moved by her love for him that he decided to resign his position as university president long before retirement age so that he could care for her himself rather than have her committed to a nursing facility. His decision was not welcomed or understood by all. Many thought he was giving up his gifts and contribution to the university and church by his decision. He always replied, "It is no sacrifice."

One time a student's wife came by to visit McQuilkin and asked him if he ever got tired of caring for his wife. His reply? "Why, no, I don't get tired. I love to care for her. She's my precious." The young woman's answer to that? "Well, I certainly would." Although he did not respond to her remark, McQuilkin summarized their continued conversation and his feelings: "Cindi and her husband are handsome, healthy, smart people, yet she admits that it is hard constantly to affirm one another. What happens when there is so little to commend? How does love make a difference?"[19]

In one congregation in a nearby state, a pastor was leading his congregation in understanding the call of the laity and their role in their workplaces, neighborhoods, and homes. He learned that I was writing this book and wanted me to come and share my ideas with his congre-

---

18. McQuilkin, "Muriel's Blessing."

19. Ibid., lines 43–53.

gation. After I gave the congregation a brief introduction to my ideas, including my call to renew the notion of testimony in public worship, I paused in my presentation and asked the people to share what God was doing in their workplaces. One woman shared about working in an after-school center trying to tutor elementary school children in reading. She described her frustration with not being able to reach them as effectively as she wished. I then asked the congregation what they should do about this. A woman across the room stood and said she knew the woman who had testified but never knew of her frustration. She now knew how to intercede for her in her efforts to help the kids learn how to read. You could hear the "amens" and the enthusiastic assent among the others in attendance. In a simple yet profound way, a congregation learned that someone was called to do something important in her workplace and they could help her by interceding in prayer for her.

After the service was over, the pastor was enthusiastic about encouraging both testimonies about workplace callings and intercessory prayer for one another as he rehearsed with me the response of the people during the service. It will require the leadership and encouragement of the pastor to make sure these things occur in public worship. Pastors are vital in healthy congregations as they carry out the mission of the church: proclaiming the gospel of Jesus Christ to the local community.

I have not forgotten the important and necessary work of administration that many pastors are expected to perform. However, is such work really necessary only for the professional minister? Is it possible that a spiritually gifted layperson might serve in administration in the local church (cf. Rom 12:8)? The pastor needs to focus on being the spiritual mentor and shepherd to the congregation. The story about the choosing of deacons in Acts 6 is important to remember. These laypeople were chosen because they were "known to be full of the Spirit and wisdom" (Acts 6:4).

I have also not forgotten the important and necessary work of being the leader in worship services. A chief characteristic of Pentecostal worship has been strong pastoral leadership. I do not quibble with this except to note that the best pastors recognize, as did John the Baptist, that "he must become greater; I must become less" (John 3:30). My great wish is that Pentecostal pastors will insist on more than just a loud worship band playing contemporary songs repeatedly as the primary point of worship, and that they will include in public worship the voices of the laity in prayers, testimonies, psalms, and spiritual songs along with the pastor's sermon. May the pastor constantly place the focus on Christ and

Christ's call to the Church to be equipped to go into the world with the gospel message backed by a gospel-formed life.

What I would like most to come from pastors is access to their callings, spiritual formation, Bible studies, and perception of the Spirit's voice. One gift that pastors can give a congregation is insight into their own pursuit of God's will and an understanding of what that means. This is not to endorse pastors' self-absorption; many would argue that there is too much of that now. Pastors should not talk about themselves all the time. My purpose, rather, is to encourage pastors to humble themselves before their congregations to reveal their very human struggles with their interior lives and their sincere desire to serve and please God in their calling. By serving as examples in this way, pastors give permission to their congregations to be honest, transparent seekers who might also long to serve and please God in their own calling. By doing this, pastors convey their unity with their congregation as together they seek to know and do God's will in their lives.

Yet another powerful gift pastors can give their congregations is permission and even encouragement for believers to seek their gifts and callings. It is empowering to know that someone with an authentic calling and gift is willing to invest time and effort in helping others find their gifts and callings. Pentecostal pastors still enjoy the respect and appreciation of their congregations—it is still a part of Pentecostal tradition to honor and deeply respect pastors. If laypeople hear their respected pastor publicly confirm their sense of call and gifting, they might enjoy a great sense of belonging. Pastors have the power to help identify and bless those whom God has gifted and called, the Spirit-filled laypeople who comprise the congregations to which they are called. Pastors' powerful voices of affirmation carry great weight.

A pastor's varied experiences and divine calling are indispensable to the training and equipping of the laity for the work of ministry. Indeed, these varied experiences and divine calling embodied by pastors should be the very kinds of qualities sought by churches as they choose their pastors (in the congregational model of church government). It is pastors who are called to train the laity for ministry in its various work, family, and neighborhood contexts. Thus, who is better to identify with a wide range of lay experiences than pastors with their own wide range of experience? Pastors with great education and personal charisma, but also with little exposure to all kinds of people in many different places—and who have little interest in such exposure—might actually be a hindrance to true pastoral ministry in the model I envision. In my view of pastoral ministry, the term *specialty* pastor—one who just wishes to preach or to counsel—is an oxymoron. The tendency of pastors and their churches is to hire specialty pastors to help pastors do the work of ministry. As church tithes (church income) rise with increased attendance, the temptation is to hire specialty pastors to assist the pastor: youth pastor, visitation pastor, worship leader, counseling pastor, etc. Why not first see if there are spiritually gifted laypeople who might fill these "specialty" roles in the church? Laypeople would be welcomed into the various ministry roles needed and more of the church's income could be freed to help the poor or for foreign missionary outreach than for professional pastoral staff salaries and benefits.

Pastors with a genuine call of God will need to continue to be curious about and attentive to all kinds of things by which they then can become better able to train the laity for ministry. "Pastoral work is first and foremost the work of enabling, teaching, helping, guiding and encouraging a specific community *to practice Christian faith themselves.*"[20] As laypeople are trained to do the work of ministry by the God-called pastor, the spiritual health of the congregation is improved and the pastor's workload is reduced so that he or she might focus on matters related to intercessory prayer, biblical studies, and the creative design of training programs for the laity to do the work of ministry.

What I hope to "say" to local pastors is not for them to have less influence, less of a "voice" to the laity. Rather, I would instead try to help them to comprehend that they can begin to train the laity to understand that they—pastor and laity—are partners in ministry. My intent is to help pastors to recognize that together they can widen their view of the landscape of lay ministry to include more than just the local church. Pastors can help to train laypeople to become lay ministers in their neighborhoods, at their worksites, and among their families. This is not to downplay the ministries of the local church—Sunday school, ushering, choir singing, etc. Rather, it is to encourage expansion of the ways and places in which laypeople can be entrusted to "do the work of ministry." It is a call to pastors to seek opportunities to become better at all kinds of things that might impact the way they help to train the laity for ministry—counseling, devotional disciplines, visitation, continuing education, family relations, social action, political awareness, and the life and spiritual transitions that various age groups will need to make.

20. Dykstra, "Imagination and the Pastoral Life," 31; (emphasis mine).

7

What Lay Ministers Can Learn
from the Missionary

. . . When God calls a people to be his people [in salvation] he calls them to join with him in his divine mission of reconciliation. This mission is both personal and social—to bring healing to individual spiritual lives through a personal relationship with God through Christ and to bring healing to the total social order. He has called the laity to be the ministers of this mission of reconciliation. Then God has given each of us a gift to enable us to serve in the area of ministry to which he calls us . . . Authentic faith is a commitment of one's life to God through Christ in a continuing and growing relationship in which one hears and understands God's call to mission, both personal and social, and gives one's self to be an instrument to fulfill this mission in the world.[1]

INTRODUCTION

A CONCERN WITH MISSIONS has been the hallmark of modern Pentecostalism since its beginnings at Azusa Street. Local churches have supported missionaries and mission stations throughout the world generously and enthusiastically. The Assemblies of God is known among Protestant churches as a foremost leader in foreign missionary efforts. Attend any Pentecostal church affiliated with any Pentecostal denomination and the chances are that missions will be a topic proclaimed boldly and unashamedly. Pentecostal laypeople are taught to give both their tithes and missionary offerings weekly and many of them are faithful to this task. Pentecostal laity also are encouraged to take short-term mission trips to help with building projects and other service-oriented missions'

---

1. Edge, "Faith and Mission," 26.

projects, usually in the developing world. Writing a check and taking a short-term trip to "foreign" places seem to be the extent of "missions" in the layperson's mind. But is there more that laypeople can "get" from the missionary and is there more that they can "do" in missions?

I am proposing that the tasks a missionary completes—adjusting to a new culture, learning the language, finding ways to serve the people, proclaiming the gospel in terms understandable to the people of that culture, establishing a solid witness for Christ by an incarnational model—are also tasks the laity should consider in their neighborhoods and/ or their workplaces. For instance, why shouldn't laypeople find ways to connect with their coworkers—speak their corporate or grassroots languages, and serve them—that will establish trusting relationships, and then, by virtue of those relationships of trust, gain a chance to share personally how the gospel has impacted their lives? Yes, this process can be risky for missionaries in hostile environments, requiring them to listen carefully to the Spirit and seek God's wisdom to do God's will in their missionary assignment. Likewise, laypeople in their workplaces may have to take some risks and will have to use great wisdom and listen to the Spirit in not violating company policies about proselytizing at work or on company time. Such things can be negotiated. I suggest that a missionary can provide a model of wisdom, courage, and Spirit call and inspiration that can benefit lay believers as they realize they are "missionaries" right where they live or work.

DEFINING THE TASK

The task of witness to a dying world must not be confined to the developing world or even only to foreign settings in the developed world. To be sure, career missionaries who are called to the developing world and other foreign settings deserve the prayers and financial support of the laity in local churches, but in every community where laypeople live, there are also places where missionary work can occur.

Instead of condemning the public schools as corrupt social experiments, would it be possible for believers to be called as teachers, guidance counselors, and administrators in the public schools? I have already shown in a previous chapter how my wife has felt such a call. However, it is disturbing to discover more and more Christian families homeschooling their children to avoid as much as possible what they have been told is an evil place. Instead of retreating or withdrawing from this setting it would be better for churches to intercede in prayer for the public schools and their Christian teachers and administrators, and to encourage the call of believers into that setting. The same might be said for politics and government service. Among many Pentecostals there can be heard loud complaints about unethical politicians and bloated, inefficient government offices and services. Instead, the church body can be encouraged to intercede and pray for our government leaders and services, and church leaders can encourage laypeople to consider whether God might be calling them to that setting.

The task is to find ways that the mission of the Church—the Great Commission—might be fulfilled not only in developing countries but also in every level of society in the developed world. For example, in North America, there is now an annual event called "Take Your Children to Work Day." It is an attempt to introduce children to their parents' work lives as well as to let them see how adult workers do their work. Why not have a similar campaign or promotion in Pentecostal churches, except this promotion might be named, "Where in the Secular Work World Might God be Calling You?" Lay believers who have sensed a call to some workplace in the secular world might be willing to allow interested young believers to view them in their work settings. The church might be able to coordinate such an event with the national effort mentioned above.

Here is the task at hand. Every day Christian laypeople go to their jobs at factories, corporations, school districts, small businesses, and government agencies. In all of these places, professional ministers—including missionaries—are most often not welcome to share their faith. In fact, in many places it is even against the law to do so. If these laypeople are there every day, then how may they serve as a kind of "missionary" in their particular setting? How may they bear witness to Christ among their fellow workers? The task for these lay Christians is to find a way to witness to and serve their coworkers. Where can they get this training and who should be their model? Using the missionary as a model, local pastors can teach laypeople ways to share the gospel with other laypeople.

Pentecostal churches have long advocated personal witness to Jesus Christ. All believers are called to testify to the saving power of the gospel in Christ. However, adequate training and modeling for that witness have often been inadequate or have been confined to the local church and the professional minister—usually the pastor or sometimes an evangelist—to provide the witness through preaching and altar call. Laypeople are only required to invite nonbelievers to church. This is getting it backwards. Ephesians 4:11 describes the gifting and calling of professional ministers. The task of these gifted professional ministers, as described in the Bible, is to "equip the saints [laypeople] for the work of ministry" (Eph 4:12 NASB). Rather than just bringing people to the church to hear the preacher give the gospel message, laypeople are to be trained and inspired by the gifted professional minister to present the gospel message where they work or in their neighborhoods.

THE TASK AND THE MISSIONARY AS MODEL

Missionaries are in a unique position to be appropriate models to laypeople who desire to influence people for Christ in their neighborhoods and workplaces. In an increasingly secularized culture where most people are biblically illiterate and many are hostile toward organized religion, a neighborhood or workplace in Western society may have the "feel" of the kind of culture evangelicals and Pentecostals are taught in church to associate with the places where missionaries are sent. In those places foreign to Western culture, missionaries are expected to *learn a new language for appropriate communication and clearer understanding, adjust to a new culture,* look for ways to *serve the people,* and *build relationships of trust over time through an incarnational model.*

In a similar fashion, laypeople in their workplaces or neighborhoods will need to build relationships of trust by the witness of their integrity and moral decisions. They will also want to find methods of serving their fellow workers or neighbors in ways in keeping with the gospel message. In addition, laypeople will need to adjust to a specific corporate culture, complete with its own corporate language. Each work setting has its own rhythms, language, employee expectations and responsibilities, and its particular emphasis. The public school setting is different from the legal setting, and each is different from the assembly line or government agency. Each setting has its unique characteristics and its unique challenges. Each one is a unique "mission field."

A word of caution is needed here. All too often, overly zealous laypeople have created resentment and even hostility by loudly and obnoxiously proclaiming a harsh or clichéd biblical message at work or in their neighborhoods instead of finding ways to connect with people. The task of sharing the gospel in the workplace is made even more difficult by prominent Christian preachers on television or radio who make strange or harsh pronouncements, which the news media love to exploit. Likewise, secular books such as James Michener's *Hawaii*, or Barbara Kingsolver's *The Poisonwood Bible*, depict missionaries who are controlling and uncaring, wanting only to enforce a harsh biblical message or impose North American practices without finding ways to serve the people, respect their culture, and build trusting relationships.[2] Thus, those missionaries or dedicated laypeople who try to connect with unreached people or neighbors or coworkers through integrity and service find themselves handicapped by caricatures of Christians as louts or legalists created in modern literature or by the news media.

In such an atmosphere, it is doubly vital for Christian laypeople to consider carefully how they may connect with their fellow workers and neighbors through their integrity and through acts of kindness and service that are true to the gospel message. The famous missiologist, Leslie Newbigin, is quite adamant about the task of missions,

> . . . a baptized congregation will not be trained *first* in churchman-
> ship [sic] and *then* in missionary responsibility . . . It will receive
> its training in churchmanship [sic] precisely in the discharge of
> its missionary responsibility.[3]

BUILDING RELATIONSHIPS OF TRUST BY AN INCARNATIONAL MODEL

Churches that encourage lay "missions" in neighborhoods and work-places may have to confront a troubling trend among believers: to remain in the church "bubble" and not view the rest of the world as worthy of Christian service. One writer sarcastically describes it this way, "[Christians] may raid the world for scalps, but they must not take a place in it."[4] To become salt and light to a dreary and dark world, Christians can take their place in it as ones who are open to trusting, caring relationships and who embody the best and most admirable qualities, both spiritual and vocational. "The gospel should enable us to become the best citizens of the world, whether as artists or homemakers

---

2. Michener, *Hawaii*; and Kingsolver, *Poisonwood Bible*.

3 Newbigin, *Household of God*, 167; (emphasis in original).

4. Stevens, *Liberating the Laity*, 97.

or scientists or politicians or educators."[5] Any relationship of trust has to begin with a sense of respect, both on the part of believers—who respect and want to serve their fellow workers and neighbors—and on the part of nonbelievers—who will naturally look on neighbors or fellow workers with greater respect and be open to meaningful relationships with them if Christian neighbors or fellow workers have the best and most admirable qualities. Christians define these qualities in reference to the fruit of the Spirit, which begins with love.[6]

Career missionaries must find ways to build trusting relationships with the nationals to whom they are sent. They are expected to embody the best and most admirable qualities, certainly, but they are also expected to be caring and accepting of people who are different from them and who might not understand their expectations.

> Since all mankind [sic] is created in the image of God, we do well to practice respect toward others. We must be aware of our tendency to reject others, and replace that attitude with one of openness and acceptance. Developing mutual respect for others has the vital potential of rewards in building good interpersonal relationships.[7]

A key to building relationships is to interpret social cues appropriately and be ready and willing to serve others sacrificially. I have tried to describe this process to my students as "incarnating" Christ's presence to people who otherwise would have no sense of what Christ's presence might mean. Recognizing the "cues" will involve emotional maturity and spiritual insight. This does not necessarily mean flashing lights, loud angelic voices raised in song, or even excited chill bumps when believers enter the workplace. It usually means that believers are the ones who volunteer to prepare a sympathy letter or card for the one who lost a loved one, buy flowers for someone in the hospital, or try to help someone with grass cutting or preparing a meal or two when sickness strikes.

Service to others must not be seen as simply tract passing or making loud demonstrations of prayer at the lunch table or displaying large Bibles prominently on one's desk. The best testimony is one of caring

---

5. Ibid., 94.

6. Note these two easily digested books that include many stories related to servanthood and the incarnational model: Elmer, *Cross-Cultural Servanthood*; and Lingenfelter and Mayers, *Ministering Cross-Culturally*.

7. Breed, *Preparing Missionaries for Intercultural Communication*, 26.

concern for others demonstrated by tangible good deeds done without fanfare and in all sincerity. An incarnational model suggests that simply being present to people with no other agenda than service and love is the key to a true and faithful witness for Christ. As representatives of Christ, Christians become the presence of Christ in whatever situation they find themselves. In this way they earn the trust of coworkers and can better find opportunities to share their faith with them.

It is easier and more convenient to produce a "witness" that is most comfortable to believers rather than to provide a kind of sacrificial service that may be very inconvenient and even difficult. It is important for the local church to make those believers interested in true lay "missions" in their neighborhoods and workplaces understand that serving others often might be difficult and require sacrifice. If "the Son of Man did not come to be served, but to serve, and to give His life as a ransom for many" (Mark 10:45), then Christians who want to be like their Lord can understand what true service might entail.

ADJUSTING TO A NEW CULTURE
AND LEARNING A NEW LANGUAGE

Career missionaries have to learn both the basics and the nuances of language to make meaningful connections with the nationals to whom they are called. In addition to the intricacies of language, they also need to negotiate the intricacies of cultural practices. Whistling in one culture is bright and cheery while in another culture it indicates someone loud and profane. The way one waves or manipulates the hand can be meaningless in one culture but have a variety of meanings in another. Wise missionaries try to decode it all before they venture out and make unforgivable blunders.

Even though lay believers might understand both the cultural nuances and intricacies of language in the dominant culture, every workplace has its own subculture and special terminology. Wise believers can learn from a missionary about how important it is to understand the corporate culture and its corporate language so that they may be effective workers and good servants of Christ in their workplace. The culture and language of teachers is different from the legal language and culture of the lawyers at the courthouse. Assembly line workers at the cookie factory have an atmosphere and corporate language different from that of assembly line workers at the auto plant.

The local church can encourage laity to try to understand and interpret properly their workplace language and subculture by having missionaries speak of their experiences in adapting to new lands and different people. In this way, missionaries give laypeople access to their journey in negotiating and interpreting language and culture. It is much more likely that a person who has worked alongside a believer and who has been in the same work culture and spoken the same work language will respond more favorably to a gospel witness from that fellow worker than from someone who is not a fellow worker. Believers who are willing to wrestle with the nuances and intricacies of language and culture in their workplaces so that they can interpret social cues appropriately will only enhance their gospel witness. Local church leadership will recognize the value of such insight by helping laypeople negotiate these nuances and intricacies.

Tom Long has a fascinating notion of how the pastor can help laypeople find the kind of language needed to share the faith.[8] It is his contention that the pastoral sermon can equip laypeople to speak honestly and personally about Jesus while still being respectful of the dignity and traditions of others. Note how he thinks this can work:

> . . . preparing to preach means thinking through how the folks in the congregation will be expected to talk and live as practical saints in the coming week. They will be involved in thousands of conversations—familial, economic, political, evangelistic, romantic—in scores of places—at work, over the backyard fence, in the mall, around the coffee pot. The sermon is an act of Christian speaking that occurs in the center of a web of gospel speech . . . When an employer calls in an employee for discipline, promotion, or dismissal, the conversation can be full of grace or it can be full of manipulation. When a teacher has a parent conference, the talk can be redemptive or deflating. When a person in the office confesses a need, the response of a co-worker can be merciful or dispassionate. If this employer, this teacher, and this co-worker sits in the pews on Sunday, the preacher has the privilege and the duty of preaching sermons that are so full of the grit of life that they model what it means to be a practical saint, an everyday preacher, one who speaks and lives the gospel.[9]

8. Long, "Preaching in the Middle of a Saintly Conversation," 15–21.

9. Ibid., 20.

While it is true that the pastor's sermon can help the laity find the language of faith in everyday life, it is also important for the pastor to hear what the laypeople are saying about the environments in which they live. Just as missionaries must understand the culture and social environment in which they live in order to find the language appropriate to that place, so pastors can learn to hear and understand the corporate culture and social settings in which the laity in their churches live.

> [Pastors] need to listen long and hard to what lay people are telling them about their environment and people's reactions to the church and Christian faith. The ordained ministry . . . needs to learn how to learn. The laity . . . should challenge the clergy to use their theological training to help them interpret within a Christian framework what they hear and experience.[10]

Likewise, visiting missionaries should be encouraged to share personal field experiences about listening carefully to the nationals' language so that they, the missionaries, might be able to connect with the nationals "where they live" and in how they think. The missionaries had to discover how to learn about the people to whom they were called just as pastors and lay ministers have to learn about the people to whom they are called.

ENCOUNTERING THE RELIGIOUS MARKETPLACE

The Christian faith has long been displaced as the prominent worldview in North America. Instead, a kind of complacent religious pluralism or weak universalism seems to be dominant. People seem to be fascinated with all sorts of religious traditions, religious movements, or even a kind of squishy personal religion entirely self-invented.[11] They appear to be increasingly unwilling to identify themselves with any one particular religious faith or tradition.[12]

While it is important to be confident in a clear understanding of one's own Christian spirituality, it is another thing to communicate that spirituality in the midst of a culture increasingly opposed to any notion of absolute truth. Before encountering the religious marketplace found in North American culture, it might be a good thing for believers to try

10. Kirk, "Sundry Thoughts on Lay Ministry," 353.

11. Blake, "Are there Dangers in being 'Spiritual but not Religious'?"

12. Ibid.

to have a basic understanding of three things: (1) Christian spirituality, (2) cultural self-awareness, and (3) a basic knowledge of other major religions.

The first item for basic understanding is this: *How is Christian spirituality properly defined* and how is it different from prevailing notions of spirituality?[13] While this might seem like a strange way to encounter other religious sensibilities—looking at oneself first—it is actually a good exercise in self-examination. Am I presenting a Christian faith that insists on always being right or being dominant? Am I exhibiting as much of the love of Christ as I am demanding the truth of Christ?

Perhaps a good question about one's spiritual life is this: What is my primary spiritual focus?[14] The best witness has to begin with one's own daily routines and rhythm of life. Do these routines work "in a sacred rhythm"?[15] If people worshiping in other religions complain about the hypocrisy or failure of Christians to exhibit any kind of religious discipline, then Christians need to understand how important are the Christian disciplines (prayer, fasting, church attendance, Bible study, etc.) and Christian discipline (the commitment to the regular practice of the disciplines) to people of other religions. Often, missionaries will need to show their seriousness about their faith in ways tangible to people of other religions. When they see how vital the missionary's faith is to him, they will show greater respect for his faith as he finds ways to speak about his faith.

There is no replacement, however, for love. A missionary can speak of her love for the people to whom she has been called. This is the center of any true spiritual transformation as well as any true Christian spiritual disciplines. "Behind discipleship and beyond the disciplines is love—love of God and love of others. Radical commitment is fine, if it is fired by love. Spiritual formation is noble, if it produces love for God and others."[16]

It is not uncommon to hear of missionaries' own personal transformation after arriving at their mission station. They are first embarrassed at their stumbling attempts to share their faith. Often a missionary will tell of some cultural mistake he has made or of his own assumption of

13. Steffen and Douglas, *Encountering Missionary Life and Work*, 62–63.

14. McKnight, "Jesus Creed," 22–24.

15. Ibid., 23.

16. Ibid.

spiritual superiority. This usually results in his becoming painfully aware of his own need for humility and transformation before attempting to transform others. Missionaries' stories about such humbling experiences are helpful to lay ministers as they encounter their own need to humble themselves before coworkers or neighbors. Lay ministers might need to consider some serious spiritual self-examination.[17]

Next, it is important to try to *understand one's cultural self-awareness*.[18] Although our motives might be pure, we might be using words or expressions that are "heard" by others in ways never intended by us. For instance, using words like "service" and "incarnating Christ" might have one meaning to Christian believers, but have a totally different meaning or no meaning to non-Christians. Also, family life or understandings of social or family arrangements might look far different to non-Christian people reared in modern North American culture and who are accustomed to no-fault divorce laws, blended families, serial marriages, living together without marriage, or even the casual use of profane language in everyday speech than they are to the much more strict interpretations of the family and social life of Christians. In trying to communicate the faith with such people, how would Christians' own understanding of the faith affect how they try to connect?

One fairly recent example of attempting to come to modern cultural awareness has to do with so many people decorating their bodies with tattoos, sometimes many of them. While this has now become a fairly routine practice among North Americans, especially young people, there are still many Christians who do not know what to make of it. Thankfully, some people are reflecting on these cultural changes and making an attempt to help Christians understand what is happening.[19] Missionaries might be helpful by relating what they have learned about interpreting what some might consider "strange" practices. Indeed, just the attempt to understand and appreciate what such practices might mean in a given culture should go a long way toward establishing a connection with people in that culture.

Missionaries can tell their stories of how they have been forced to interpret just what is going on in the societies to which they have been called. Peering into the life of a different culture, missionaries have dis-

---

17. See Taylor, "Changing Your Mind."

18. Hesselgrave, *Communicating Christ Cross-Culturally*, 105.

19. Paulsell, "Body Language," 18–24.

covered their own cultural ignorance or prejudices. Besides having to interpret the societies they have entered, they also have to interpret the ways they have reacted and felt about those societies. They have learned that the way they feel about that society and its mores has a tremendous effect upon the way they interpret what is going on and helps them to discover what they should be doing.

Finally, it is important to have at least *a rudimentary knowledge of the different religions that have become popular for North Americans.*[20] Lumping Muslims, Hindus, Buddhists, Sikhs, and New Age adherents into one large group of "sinners" fails to show respect to each group and speaks of Christian arrogance. How can Christians expect to be heard and respected if they do not listen and respect others in their faiths or religious sensibilities? This does not mean having to accept as true what the others are saying about their faith; it is simply a matter of showing proper respect. While it might be argued that Paul was not very success-ful in terms of numbers of converts when he visited the Areopagus, it cannot be argued that he did not show respect for the religion(s) of the Athenians (Acts 17:16–34, cf. v. 22).

Sadly, sometimes people in other religions are much more aware of Christian beliefs and the Christian Bible than are many Christians. Missionaries can tell stories of their surprise at finding many people to whom they were called who were familiar with the Bible and able to recite portions of it. They can also tell of how important it is for them to know what the Bible says, finding ways to interpret it to the new culture in ways appropriate to the biblical story and the culture. As one writer put it, "Trust the stories. Trust the God in the stories."[21] It is hard to do that if Christians themselves don't know the stories. It is also very embarrassing to learn that people of other religions just might know the Christian Bible better than they.

In describing how they dealt with the religious marketplace among the nationals to whom they were sent, these missionaries can now help lay ministers to articulate the gospel message clearly. They can help to train lay ministers in how to bring a person to faith in Jesus Christ. While it is important to serve others, respect other's faith, and know the biblical stories, it is also very important to know how to lead others to Christ and to have the courage to do so. Besides the importance of sensitivity and

20. Steffen and Douglas, *Encountering Missionary Life and Work*, 63–64.

21. Swenson, "Biblically Challenged," 22–25.

knowledge about these various things, nothing can replace a knowledge of and sensitivity to the work of the Spirit. Appealing to the Spirit is no excuse not to learn the most and the best that can be learned about how to serve and care for others, but no learning can replace the work of the Holy Spirit in leading believers in just the right way of doing the work of ministry.

THE WORK OF THE HOLY SPIRIT

No one with any understanding of Christian witness in any setting—lay or professional—can ignore the importance of being filled with the Holy Spirit and learning the discipline of listening to and obeying the voice of the Spirit. As with ministry in general, it must be understood that access to the Spirit is not limited to the professional minister. Not everyone baptized in the Spirit on the Day of Pentecost recorded in Acts 2:4 was called by God to be an apostle, prophet, evangelist, or pastor, yet all were encouraged to wait until the Spirit was poured out for power for witness (Acts 1:4, 8). Again, as with a call, the best thing professional ministers can do is give the laity access to their experience of the Spirit as well as help them in their quest to hear and recognize the voice of the Spirit.

Missionaries can be invited to the local church to describe their experiences with the guidance of the Spirit and how that was expressed in the ways they served the people to whom they were sent. Time can be given for laypeople to ask the missionaries questions about their experience in relation to issues or struggles laypeople might be having. Wise pastors will be sensitive to the concerns of laypeople so that they are strengthened and encouraged in their communion with God by the Holy Spirit.

This communion with the Spirit is necessary for several reasons. Believers need to be strengthened for their ministry work. They also need the Spirit to help them as they pray for their coworkers, neighbors, and family members. The Spirit can help believers find the courage to do the work of ministry in strange and/or hostile environments. Perhaps most importantly, the Spirit can sustain believers through times of discouragement and disappointment. All of these experiences with the Spirit can be described by visiting missionaries who have needed just such sustenance from the Holy Spirit.

Both missionaries and pastors can be repositories of wisdom and Spirit confirmation for the situations laypeople may face in their workplaces and neighborhoods. Since it is wise to get confirmation before acting on what we think to be direction from the Spirit, wise pastors and missionaries might help believers with that confirmation. At the very least, local pastors can develop a network of lay church leaders who can be trusted with their connection to and understanding of the voice of the Spirit so that all can find someone to help in these important spiritual matters.

Releasing the work of listening to the Spirit and the work of confirmation of the Spirit to committed lay leaders might be fraught with potential difficulties for local pastors, but by risking this, pastors might very well see the abundant fruit of true ministry in a dark world desperate for loving, Spirit-filled people who demonstrate their concern in tangible ways.

MISSION TRIPS

An important part of the Pentecostal experience in the Assemblies of God is the short-term mission trip. The Assemblies of God has always encouraged laypeople to visit mission stations and help missionaries in foreign countries. The practice of short-term mission trips has not waned. In fact, these trips might be even more important.

> The concept of sending mission teams for short-term work has grown increasingly popular in U.S. congregations. People are not excited about sending their dollars off to faceless mission agencies; they want to become personally involved. Encouraged by the testimony of others who have had life-changing experience in a Third World country, they want to 'do mission' themselves.[22]

It is this kind of lay interest in missions that helps Assemblies of God missions continue to be among the best in the world. A good short-term mission trip helps laypeople appreciate the work and sacrifice of the missionaries whom they support.

The downside of short-term mission work is that laypeople might pick and choose projects to support rather than to view the "big picture" in terms of the overall work of the missionary.[23] This only creates more pressure on missionaries to raise their support when they return to the U.S. for itineration. Also, laypeople have a tendency to want to

22. Jeffery, "Short-term Mission Trips," 5.
23. Ibid.

"do" something tangible while they are there are on the mission field, such as constructing a building or conducting services through an interpreter rather than simply observing, listening, and connecting with the nationals.[24] This can put the missionary in an uncomfortable position of having to accommodate the visiting laypeople by finding the projects they are most willing to do rather than the laypeople trying to accommodate the missionary's schedule and agenda. In addition to that, when the missionary itinerates, he might be expected to highlight the work of the lay "helpers" who visited his mission station when he appeals for more funds for his budget. Thus, his itineration becomes mostly about money and budgets and happy, giving laypeople rather than about his burden for his field of service or about what kinds of things the missionary might be able to teach laypeople.

I would never suggest the end of short-term mission trips. If they are planned well, laypeople can enjoy a life-changing experience. What I would suggest is an expansion of the role of the itinerating missionary. It might be called a kind of short-term mission trip in reverse in that instead of laypeople only going to the missionary where she is stationed, she is also invited to come to local churches to testify about her work, her struggles, her successes, her joys, and her frustrations. She can be the sounding board for lay ministers who are "missionaries" in settings in North American culture that need a gospel witness.

The short-term mission trips I envision have the church funding a trip for the missionary to come to that church to help train them in their own missionary work in their community. Yes, the missionary could raise money for his budget while he is there, but he would be mainly a resource person to help laypeople understand that they, too, are missionaries, saying, "Here are the issues you need to consider in your lay 'missionary' ministry."

LAYPEOPLE AS MISSIONARIES

In his study of lay ministry, J. Andrew Kirk has listed certain characteristics of a missionary church.[25] These qualities of missionaries should characterize the laity as they are sent into their corporate or family "worlds" with a gospel witness. The first characteristic he lists is *pilgrim*.

---

24. Radecke, "Misguided Missions," 22–23, 25.
25. Kirk, "Sundry Thoughts on Lay Ministry," 345–62.

By this he means that the faith community is one that is "exploring and crossing new frontiers, a community on the move, anxious to face new challenges and to find new ways of fulfilling its calling."[26] I would suggest that focusing on the corporate, governmental, and public school arenas (among many that could be mentioned) would constitute "new" challenges for many Pentecostal churches that have been far too insular and self-serving. Many Pentecostal believers have not considered that they might be commissioned and trained as lay ministers to be sent to "new" frontiers. After all, public schools, government offices, and corporate entities are often condemned as "worldly," "secular," and evil instead of being viewed as places of genuine Christian (missionary!) service.

The second characteristic of a missionary church is that it is *engaging with the world*. By this Kirk means that laypeople "contextualize" in appropriate ways the message of the gospel in places where they live and work every day.[27] Believers do not go "into" the world as if they are crossing an invisible line between sacred and secular space. Their church is already in the world as a gospel witness. Since laypeople are there already, it only makes sense to engage with their "world" and the language and social cues appropriate to it. This "engagement" with their "world" will mean they will incarnate God's presence there with "the fragrance of Christ" (2 Cor 2:14–16).[28]

The third characteristic of a missionary church is that it *takes risks*. Indeed, living out the faith in the world is a risky business since believers will face challenges from the world, the flesh, and the devil (cf. 1 John 2:15–17).

> [The church's calling] may be to defend unpopular causes, take the side of minorities, confront powerful interest groups, mediate in violent situations, care for people with highly contagious diseases or suffering from natural disasters; all highly risky situations (other instances of the life of faith are given in Hebrews 11).[29]

Courage is needed to provide a witness where none existed before. It takes even more courage to provide a witness where a bad one has existed before. A missionary might risk life, limb, or visa to take certain

---

26. Ibid., 350.

27. Ibid., 350–51.

28. Ibid., 351.

29. Ibid., (parenthesis in original).

risks in her missionary duties. A lay minister might risk unemployment or harsh discipline for taking a principled stand or obeying the promptings of the Spirit in her work environment. She might have to overcome bad experiences coworkers have had with obnoxious or "carnal" Christians either as former coworkers or from their past.

Lastly, a missionary church will be *compassionate*. Kirk has defined it this way:

> [It is] a willingness to be available to others as they may require support, encouragement, the use of particular skills or someone to whom they can express anger, remorse, or sorrow. Compassion must not be confused with charitable duty, condescension, philanthropy or beneficence. It is manifested in "waiting upon," in both senses of the word.[30]

It is good to remember the times the Gospels speak of Christ's compassion for those he encountered and what that meant for those people (Matt 9:36; 14:14; Mark 1:41; 6:34). As Christ's disciples, the compassion of Christ can be evident in the ways believers serve others. A believer can ask, "In what ways may I incarnate Christ's compassion to my coworkers, neighbors, or family members?"

These fine qualities are ones to which laypeople might aspire as they learn from missionaries about these very things. As missionaries tell their stories, laypeople can learn from their experiences, ask them questions, and join them in their prayers. In these ways, missionaries "communicate" to laypeople their hearts, wisdom, and actions.

I hope the time will come when local churches and their professional ministers are ready to equip and help sustain laypeople as missionaries in their workplaces and neighborhoods. These laypeople may very well be the only "ministers" nonbelievers ever encounter in an increasingly secularized or pluralistic North American culture. Since that is probably the case already, it is urgent for the laypeople who are already there—and are there every day—to be ready and willing to meet their responsibilities. It is no longer appropriate simply to say to the laypeople, "You need to be a witness in this world." They already know that. They want to be affirmed, trained, encouraged, sustained, and recognized as fellow ministers of the gospel. May it happen soon.

30. Ibid., 351–52.

8

A Wisdom Movement Needed

Wisdom is a surprising resource for the continual reexamination of Israel's faith. The wise man in his method sought to be always in dialogue with the reality of his environment. He was always curious about the intricacies of his social order, the delicacy of human relationship, the marvel and mystery of his natural environment. He always wanted to know. He would not settle for yesterday's answers but asked how it looked today. . . . Faith can become a way to work the system, to explain life, and to manipulate for our own ends. Theology can become safe and respectable so that it is the announcement of yesterday's authenticities in the face of new realities, the parroting of old certainties, the defense of old positions, the insistence upon old questions, the passion to make events and persons fit the scheme of how they are supposed to be . . . Proverbs . . . is an example of a style of life in which men [sic] really ask about the message given in their environment. In such a dialogue nothing is trivial or safely ignored. Each small turn of events speaks a word to us and discloses a freshness about the world in which we live. The word spoken is often a new word, unexpected, not in conformity with how we thought it should be and always was. Proverbs thus embodies an approach to life of disciplined curiosity which we may call "scientific": wanting to know about the world in which we live and the resources available to us. The method of such inquiry, when properly done, involves waiting for new disclosures, being attentive and responsible to them, and receiving them when they come, even if it means the abandonment of what was precious and had seemed true.[1]

CONVERSATIONS OF SUBSTANCE

LONG, THE FAMOUS NEW Testament and Homiletics scholar, tells this story:

1. Brueggemann, *In Man We Trust*, 115–16.

On a trip to the Holy Land several years ago, I was amused to find, posted over the doorway of the little church near the Garden of Gethsemane, a sign reading, "No explanations allowed in the Church!" Presumably this message was intended to prevent the drone of tour guides from spoiling the mood in the lovely sanctuary, but it could well serve, by extension, as a warning to excessively didactic preachers everywhere who attempt to connect the hipbone of sanctification to the thighbone of predestination, to provide exploding diagrams of the Trinity, and to pop the crystal off the face of the Christian calendar to expose the gears and springs.[2]

However interesting, fruitful, helpful, painful, tedious, or boring good discussions might be, they are still necessary and even vital to the life of faith. Far too many believers do not engage in discussions of substance, preferring instead to "keep it light," impersonal. However, it is only through conversations and discussions of depth and meaning that real change, real spiritual growth can occur. The phrase, "keep it real," suggests transparency, authenticity, and depth of relationship. It can also turn into a cliché[set acute accent over e], a convenient verbal attempt to keep people at arm's length rather than actually practicing authenticity where the potential risks of having to listen and participate in meaningful discussions is required.

Even having a "polite" conversation about important issues related to faith, personal discipline, godly service to others, and social action might be difficult and frustrating in and of itself. Many seem to have firm opinions based on personal feelings and agendas, while others have practiced well the art of indifference and complacency. Still others are content to allow favorite radio and television pundits tell them what to think and say. Often, the radio and television pundits rely on ratings to keep their sponsors and stay on the air. As a result, they usually appeal to human anger about some political or social issue to stir up their audiences and thus keep them tuned in. Sadly, this can turn otherwise godly people into hateful and angry sycophants of their favorite pundits.

On the other hand, many people just don't want to be bothered with issues of depth and meaning. They might argue that they attend church services to "get" something for themselves with little concern for others. Like good consumers, they "shop" for the "best" church services

2. Long, "Struggling Toward Ash Wednesday," 25–31.

to get from those services just what they need and have little or nothing to do with fellow believers sitting right next to them in church. Having nothing to contribute and wanting only to take for themselves from the church service, they are not interested in working to develop relationships of wisdom, meaning, and depth. Some might sympathize with this description of the local church provided by Eugene Peterson upon taking his first pastorate:

> The people who gathered to worship God under my leadership were rootless and cultureless. They were marginally Christian. They didn't read books.   They didn't discuss ideas. All spirit seemed to have leaked out of their lives and been replaced by a garage-sale clutter of clichés and stereotypes, securities and fashions. . . . It was a marshmallow culture, spongy and without substance. . . . I was thirty years old and had never experienced this blandness, this willingness to be homogenized into passive consumerism. . . . In a fast-food culture they came to church for fast-religion help. Hanging around them all week long, I was in danger of reducing my idea of them to their self-concepts.[3]

To achieve the formation of wise and caring people in the faith community requires laypeople who want to learn, discuss, and pray about what it might mean to be persons of meaning, depth, and true spirituality. If believers are not interested in sound Christian teaching and authentic spirituality, then what are their interests? The "quality" of the worship band? The "excitement" of the church service? The charisma of the preacher? The size of the youth group? The facilities in the nursery? With such primary concerns as these, how can an atmosphere of godly wisdom and true spirituality develop?

Perhaps all of this simply reflects an inability to be able to engage in discussions of meaning and depth because of ignorance. Maybe people just need to learn how to discuss matters of meaning and depth courteously. This might mean more time in church settings in which pastors and worship leaders are silent while laypeople are given a chance to speak. Also, modeling might be used to "explain" what good conversations or discussions might entail. For instance, some churches may often use panel discussions led by the pastor on Sunday morning in lieu of the sermon. In these settings, designated laypeople sit on stage and engage in a lengthy discussion with the pastor on some significant subject.

3. Peterson, *Under the Predictable Plant*, 61–62.

Periodically during the panel discussion, people in the congregation are allowed to ask the panelists questions about their discussion. In this scenario three things are happening:

1. Believers see that meaningful discussions about important issues can occur.

2. They learn how to discuss things courteously with other believers.

3. They discover that matters of depth and meaning are not just the concern of professional ministers.

This is not to suggest that we do not need the work of professional ministers and religious scholars. Indeed, their work is vital to the life of the church. For instance, the work of deciding about Christian doctrine and the human spiritual condition is the work of a theologian. We need theologians to help us see how God's plan of salvation is unfolding in light of the word of God. We need theologians to judge the way the Church formulates its proclamation and lives out its faith.

While all believers need to know and practice good theology, not all of us can be theologians. Instead, I would propose that we become sages. Sages can be professional ministers and scholars as well as wise laypeople regardless of formal education. A sage can be one who knows God and good theology but who would be more comfortable observing and appreciating creation and the human person and situation. To summarize subjects from Proverbs, sages know that insects, young people, home life, and even politicians can teach us something.

THE NEED FOR SAGES

I would thus propose a kind of new wisdom tradition among us that recognizes our accumulated wisdom in light of our deep and abiding faith. In other words, we need to understand that there can be a kind of sage-like witness among us that models a new openness to dialogue, a new appreciation for the abilities of humankind, recognition of the accomplishments throughout history of great people in all walks of life that have changed the course of human history. As sages, we can all be careful observers, willing conversationalists, founts of insight and knowledge about both our disciplines and the mysterious ways of God in our vocations.

The sages in Proverbs could speak of divine activity in humanity with little reference to God. It is true that the beginning of wisdom is the fear of God (Prov 9:10), but innate in creation exists a divine wisdom that can be observed and appreciated. It takes a sage to recognize it, bring it to light, and teach others about the benefits of such sagacity, which is really open to all. I want to be a sage, a wise person who knows how to observe, converse, appreciate, and enjoy what God has provided in every area of life, in every discipline we teach.

Our efforts to become sages do not mean that the role of evangelist has been abandoned. Perhaps we could say the role has been broadened and enriched by observing and appreciating the wisdom discovered in humans and their vocations. A wise person will know the language of the businessman or social worker. A wise person will appreciate the benefits of good politics and society. A wise person will be thankful for the little bit of heaven provided by the earnest and well-trained musician. Observing, appreciating, and learning the language of these professions does not make us less able to do evangelism. Indeed, such activity on our part may very well make us even better evangelists, when the situation calls for it.

On the other hand, if the only reason we wish to observe and learn about various professions and those who practice those professions is to share our faith with them, I am confident they will see through our little scheme and be put off by our utilitarianism. If, however, we are "there" with them, appreciating sincerely what they do, hearing their passions about what they do, and learning their language, the opportunity for sharing God's love will happen quite naturally. But even if it does not, we will at least learn that God can work in creation and in people in ways that we have failed to appreciate before. In his classic work, *All Truth Is God's Truth*, Arthur Holmes put it this way:

> The Christian should approach the present life constructively, seeking peace and reconciliation with others rather than pursuing selfish interests or allowing alienation to persist (Col 3:5–16). He should work wholeheartedly at his family relationships and economic tasks, for these too are a part of God's mandate to his creatures (Col 3:17–4:1).[4]

---

4. Holmes, *All Truth Is God's Truth*, 11.

SOME BACKGROUND

The Hebrew word from which the English word for wisdom is derived is *hokma* or "skill."[5] It was used in the Bible in connection with the ability of artisans (Exod 31:30), but for the wisdom-writers it referred to skill in living (Prov 13:24), with political leaders (Prov 22:29), in work (Prov 13:11; 14:23–24, 31:10–19), and with other people (Prov 17:27).[6] Wisdom in Hebrew referred to the practical skill (*hokma*) of a craftsman (see Exod 35:30—36:1, especially 35:35) and to various trades.[7] But wisdom can also refer to cleverness in dealing with life's situations. "The Hebrew term (for 'wisdom') and its cognate (for 'wise') . . . might be said to describe the art of being successful."[8]

But this does not necessarily mean the kind of success we think of in North American culture. Although material prosperity was one of the Hebrews' major concerns, the wisdom literature emphasizes righteousness and ethical behavior. A better term for "success" might be "contentment" or even "satisfaction in life."

It follows, then, that for believers to discover contentment in life they must study individual and social behavior. This is why Hebrew wisdom is "essentially practical."[9] We might even call Hebrew wisdom a study in human experience. H.W. Robinson has said here, " . . . the wisdom of Israel [is] the discipline whereby was taught the application of prophetic truth to the individual life in the light of experience."[10]

But human experience was not the only source of wisdom. It is true that the wisdom-teachers appealed to both the wise dealing and the foolishness of human behavior as sources of knowledge and proof for their teachings. Yet true wisdom found its source in God. However, one must not forget the appeal of wisdom-teaching (especially in Proverbs) to seek out wisdom by human effort and diligence. Roland Murphy has made a good point here:

> It may be helpful for the reader to think of these aspects of wisdom, divine and human, as divine summons and human re-

5. Martens, *God's Design*, 166.

6. Ibid., 180.

7. Bullock, *Introduction to the Old Testament Poetic Books*, 21.

8. Harrison, *Introduction to the Old Testament*, 1007.

9. Ibid.

10. H. W. Robinson, *Inspiration and Revelation in the Old Testament*, 241.

sponse. From the point of view of Wisdom's divine origin, she speaks for God, inviting [people] to life. From the other point of view, wisdom is also that response which human beings are to make to the summons by their wise conduct.[11]

If a person would seek out and find the divine wisdom given to humankind, this wisdom could then be practically applied. It is true that wisdom's source was God and wisdom's pursuit was reverence for God. But after receiving this wisdom, a person could use it in every area of life. Harrison has said here:

> The inscrutable nature of divine wisdom was such that man needed a revelation of divine grace if he was to grasp it at all (Job 28:23, 28), but given this it was possible for the insights of wisdom to be applied to all works of life.[12]

Murphy has suggested, "'Coping with life,' not 'mastery of life' seems a more accurate description of the goal of the sages who remained aware of life's mysteries."[13] On the other hand, Martens has said, " . . . wisdom [for the Hebrew] [was] skill in living. Wisdom deals with mastery of life."[14] It begs the question for modern interpreters: Is everything figured out for us, or are we given skills to deal with whatever issue arises? Indeed, we would do well to ponder the notion of so many people in our culture who promise all the answers to life's questions—both within the church through preachers' recorded series on seven steps to success or in the secular world with business, real estate, or personal growth seminars. In light of the competing notions of having just the right formula to be successful versus having the necessary skills to handle what life brings us, sages can provide some kind of response that is true to the biblical text and the way things really are in the nitty-gritty world in which we live.

SOME POTENTIAL DANGERS

Good sages provide Spirit-enabled wisdom to the community of the faithful so that they are guarded against three potential dangers. The first danger is unrestrained self-absorption disguised as "freedom in Christ."

11. Murphy, *Wisdom Literature and Psalms*, 35.

12. Harrison, *Introduction to the Old Testament*, 1008.

13. Murphy, *Wisdom Literature and Psalms*, 29.

14. Martens, *God's Design*, 166.

Some people believe heaven itself bows before their selfish agendas and personal opinions. Instead of hearing good wisdom, they might respond by saying, "I don't receive that," as if so saying negates its truth. Or, they might say in response to a call to right action or holy living, "I don't yet feel convicted about that," as if the life of faith were optional for them.

The second potential danger is legalism or the temptation to promote a mechanical understanding of God's work. This usually means people are impatient with the complexities of life and the modern world or are unwilling to expend the energy required to pray, study, and listen for the voice of the Spirit as they discern God's truth in a complex world. They are more comfortable consulting a rulebook or subscribing strictly to a particular theological perspective regardless of how the Spirit might be working or how truthful another perspective might be.

The last potential danger is an uncritical trust in "technology." After all, if there is a problem we can just bring in the best "expert," or read the latest "how to" book, or project the latest technological wonder onto the problem, correct? Of course, the problem with this is that technology by itself cannot discern the human element. "How to" books might have some good ideas, but they fail to anticipate the nuances and complexities found in different communities, each with its own set of strengths and weaknesses. The "cookie-cutter" approach has never worked. While all these "solutions" may be helpful, none of them can replace Spirit-enabled discernment by gifted sages. The Spirit may actually lead believers to stand *against* the latest bestseller, "authoritative" expert, or best technological wizardry.

However, let me quickly add that modern technology can be helpful and, when used properly, can enhance the life of the community. I have already mentioned in chapter 3 how larger churches might be able to make good use of videos during commissioning services. There is, however, a danger in relying too much on video presentations and losing the spontaneity of the moment. Again, wisdom from sages will be needed.

I also recognize that it might be helpful to connect with younger people through online personal posting sites (e.g., Facebook, Twitter, and even through text messages). Indeed, there has been such a preoccupation with these things among younger believers that some churches are calling for "technology fasts," during which all are asked to set aside the latest technology for a prescribed period and devote that time to personal devotions and face-to-face fellowship. This might be a good practice to be enacted regularly by churches. Nevertheless, the proper use of the latest technology can be implemented with the wisdom provided by church sages and the work of the Spirit.

THE GREAT NEED FOR WISDOM

In all of my proposals for finding God's call to lay ministry, developing true fellowship, following the missionary model, etc., I would have to insist on the necessary ingredient of wise elders and mentors for the whole process of developing both a healthy and supportive church atmosphere and for sustaining laypeople in their various callings in their workplaces, neighborhoods, and families. Identifying wise lay leaders is vitally important, but it is also important to identify the *kind* of wisdom that is being dispensed.

The Epistle of James describes the right kind of wisdom "from above" (Jas 3:13–18) as well as the end result of the right kind of wisdom. But what impresses me most in this passage is the mention of good fruit and sincerity. Sincere lay believers whose lives produce the good fruit of the Spirit and who have a fruitful lay ministry are the ones who should be considered for the role of sage in the church. This testimony concerning wise believers should come from others who have observed their lives over a significant period of time. Wise people are *mature* in the faith (Heb 5:14).

In the Epistle to the Hebrews, the writer is frustrated with the people. He wants to impart some wisdom in his teaching but believes them to be disinterested (Heb 5:11–12). They do not even have a grasp of elementary truths, much less of in-depth knowledge of God's Word (Heb 5:12–13). Because it is easy to encounter so many believers who are likewise disinterested, it is easy to become as frustrated with them as was the writer of the Epistle with those early believers. Instead of expressing their frustration, however, pastors and local church leaders might highlight wise laypeople as models and invite others into a deeper and more meaningful understanding of the faith through conversations with believers who are considered wise in the true, biblical way.

To accomplish these goals, professional ministers will have to share the role of wise leader with key laypeople—men and women—as well as to put an emphasis on a higher, better, and more meaningful life of faith. Pastors can learn much from wise lay leaders, both men and women.

Pastors and wise lay leaders will need courage to resist calls from some in their churches for more church entertainment and an unhealthy reliance upon prepackaged church programs. Hearing what the Spirit is saying to their local churches—a message not communicated by entertainment or prepackaged programs—will require the leadership of wise pastors and laypeople as they seek God together. Sages will know what is truly valuable to their faith communities and will seek to emphasize those things instead of other things that are vacuous, sensual, or that overtly endorse one political view over another.

It will take wise people to know what is truly important to the life of faith and be able to discern the fresh wind of the Spirit blowing in a particular direction. This might also mean that these wise people will have to point out what only cleverly masquerades as the wind of the Spirit. These cleverly disguised movements, fads, or social programs might make grandiose promises and be packaged in appealing ways, but in the final analysis, they are not appropriate for believers or their local church.

With a fairly modern history of failed television ministers and misguided "movements," including so-called "revival" movements, it is usually fairly easy to give a "wise" word of caution to those who might get caught up in an updated version of a corrupt preacher or an alleged "revival." It is important to "discern the signs of the times" (Matt 16:3). It is not so easy to discern that what might be taken for granted by people as proper or true might yet also be harmful.

One example of something harmful to believers that is often thought to be proper is the insidious way North American culture is becoming so driven, so addicted to "busyness." Our schedules and agendas are too tightly wound, requiring such expert juggling that we are left exhausted and spent at the end of every day. Who has time to rest when there is this or that still unfinished on our list of chores—groceries to buy, bathrooms to clean, dishwasher to empty, clothes to be washed, bills to pay, kids to taxi, lawns to care for, church activities to attend? Believers could take that addiction to "busyness" and apply it to their lay ministries, driving themselves into exhaustion and/or depression—I did too much or I didn't do enough!

A woman went on vacation with her daughter and workaholic son-in-law, a man who was always working or obsessing about his work. She reported that as they were lounging by the pool, trying to enjoy much needed rest, the son-in-law, a builder, used his cell phone to try to reach his salespeople. After several unsuccessful attempts, he finally reached his office and asked, "Tell me something, am I the only one working today?!"

Is there a wise word from sages in local churches who have the courage to say to the busy person, "Take a Sabbath rest!"? Would that busy person believe the sages? And what other not-so-obvious issues thought to be true are yet causing harm to believers?

For all things—obvious and not so obvious—the church needs sages, people who are attuned to the Scriptures and to the wind of the Spirit. To paraphrase Qoheleth (the preacher) in Ecclesiastes 3, there is a time to resist "busyness" and life's many pressures and a time to respond appropriately; there is a time to work and a time to play; there is a time to stand firmly on clear convictions and a time to be silent and listen. Our times are in God's hands (Ps 31:15). Wise people know what time it is.

9

Final Thoughts

We need large institutional churches because the vast majority of Christians will not be able to live highly intentional lives. And we need celibate monasteries both to keep us connected to our pre-Reformation heritage and to provide an honored place for those not called to marriage.

Above all we need something that does not now exist—places where those called to greater intentionality can connect with others who have received the same call, and where together they can give each other the support needed to carry out that call.[1]

ALL OF MY PROPOSALS taken together will require much energy and intentionality, perhaps more than many Pentecostals are willing to give. However, many other Pentecostals will feel compelled to find communities in which my proposals might be implemented. Where will they find these communities? How will these communities be formed and maintained?

Jonathan Wilson-Hartgrove argues that there is a hunger among Western believers at the beginning of the twenty-first century for the ways in which ancient monastic communities provided alternative places of witness to the radical teachings of Christ. In fact, he says, "Much of the Protestant Reformation was driven by the monastic impulse. Nowhere is this clearer than in the radical Reformation that gave rise to Quakers, Shakers, Baptists, *Pentecostals*, evangelicals, and other radical Christian groups."[2]

---

1. Kauffman, "Evangelicals and Monastics," 32.
2. Wilson-Hartgrove, "A Vision so Old it Looks New," 16; (emphasis mine).

If believers respond in intentional ways to my proposals about discovering God's call and forming communities of God-called people who practice hospitality, nurture, and fellowship with wisdom, there will have to be a radical reorientation of how believers understand the Christian faith and its practices. "Nothing is more characteristic of monastic and evangelical groups than their unshakable belief that one cannot be truly spiritual without putting one's faith into practice, and one cannot sustain Christian discipleship without a prayerful spirituality."[3]

It is not my intention to advocate the erection of monasteries wherein believers might hide away from worldly corruption or the influence of worldly and less-intentional believers. Rather, the whole witness of the best of monastic community life—a shared rule of life, a common purpose, an emphasis on community and love, the stated goal of combining prayer and work—is something to which the best Pentecostal communities should aspire. "Jesus Christ calls us to a shared and common life in him. Since most church members have no idea such a life exists, much less is desirable, it is imperative that we look for models of what it could be—as in new monastic communities."[4]

Western culture with its worship of technology and individuality is opposed to a shared life in which people learn to "submit to one another . . . " (Eph. 5:21). If there is hostility to the formation of caring, covenantal communities committed to radical response to God's spirit, then that hostility can be traced directly to the notion of individualism deep within the DNA of Americans. "Church members, as individuals, are easy pickings for the Powers of Death; they will separate us, isolate us, dismember us, pick us off one at a time, and grind us down into the dust."[5]

In forming communities of Pentecostals radically committed to following God's call as the Spirit leads into all parts of Western society, there has to be an emphasis on a common life, a deeply shared purpose. This shared purpose is discovered in the work of the Spirit as revealed on the Day of Pentecost as described by Acts 2. Believers empowered by God's spirit were united around sound teaching, prayer, fellowship, and shared meals (Acts 2:42). Here is how one pastor described a caring, intentional church community:

3. Kauffman, "Evangelicals and Monastics," 30.

4. Childress, "Ties that Bind," 35.

5. Ibid., 39.

"I want my people to think in terms of God and each other, each other and God—that we cannot have one without the other—and to think like this so much that it becomes habitual."[6]

Until believers are willing to form intentional communities that have agreed to the same practices ("habits"), any proposals—not just mine—will only serve as fads in a long line of novelties in which Western believers have dabbled for a while. I cannot fulfill my call without others who love, forgive, and support me. I must be able to count on this love, forgiveness, and support. If such qualities are only fleeting or offered insincerely, I will be discouraged and hindered in my response to the work of the Spirit.

My radical call in this book is to form communities in which my proposals become the "habit" around which all in the community will rally. With these proposals for a sense of call, an empowered community, hospitality, nurture, fellowship, testimony, and wisdom, believers can form a community that makes plain how the members live out the Christian faith and how they love and serve one another. We can regularly say to one as we share the sacred meal, "The Body of Christ," recognizing that we are the Body of Christ formed by the spirit of Christ. Perhaps such a community, one day, might be able to say to others (paraphrasing the Apostle Paul), "Whatever you have learned or received or heard from [us], or seen in [us]—put it into practice. And the God of peace will be with you" (Phil 4:9).

6. Ibid.

Bibliography

Akinwale, Anthony. "Dignity, Diversity, and Complemenarity: The Lay Faithful in the Ecclesiology of Pope John Paul II." *Nova et Verita* 3, no. 4 (2003) 651–72.

Althouse, Peter. Review of *Invading Secular Space: Strategies for Tomorrow's Church*, by Martin Robinson and Dwight Smith. *The Pneuma Review* 11, no. 4 (Fall 2008).

Amit, Yairah. *Reading Biblical Narratives*. Nashville: Abingdon/Fortress, 2001.

Anameje, Humphrey Chinedu. "Contemporary Theological Reflection on the Laity: Towards a More Active Participation in the Mission of the Church." *Journal of Ephemerides Theologicae Lovanienses* 83, no. 4 (2007) 445–70.

Anderson, Robert C. "In Search of the Disabled Human Body in Theological Education: Critical Perspective on the Construction of Normalcy and Overview." *Journal of Religion* 56, no. 3 (2008).

Arulsamy, S. "The Urgency of Promoting Lay Leadership in Emerging India." Art. 2. *Vidyajyoti Journal of Theological Reflection* 69 (2005) 500–13.

Atkinson, Gordon. "How to Find a Church." *Christian Century* (November 16, 2004) 10.

———. "The Listening Place: An Encounter with Quaker Spirituality." *Christian Century* (February 23, 2010) 12–13.

Banks, Robert. "The Community as a Loving Family." In *Paul's Idea of Community*, rev. ed. Peabody, MA: Hendrickson, 1994.

Banks, Robert, and R. Paul Stevens. *The Complete Book of Everyday Christianity*. Downers Grove, IL: InterVarsity, 1997.

Barclay, William. *The Letters to the Corinthians in the Daily Study Bible*. Atlanta: Westminster/John Knox, 1956.

Becker, Amy Julia. "An Hour with Penny: Encountering Down Syndrome." *Christian Century* (January 12, 2010) 10.

Betenbaugh, Helen. "Disability: A Lived Theology." *Theology Today* 57, no. 2 (2000) 203–10.

Blake, John. "Are there any dangers in being 'Spiritual but not Religious'?" CNN (June 9, 2010). Online: http://www.cnn.com/2010/LIVING/personal/06/03/spiritual.but.not.religious/index.html?iref=allsearch.

Blumhofer, Edith L. *The Assemblies of God, Pentecostalism, and American Culture*. Champaign: University of Illinois Press, 1993.

Boers, Arthur. "What Henri Nouwen Found at Daybreak." *Christianity Today* 38, no. 11 (October 3, 1994) 28–31.

Breed, Layman E. *Preparing Missionaries for Intercultural Communication: A Bicultural Approach*. Pasadena, CA: William Carey Library, 1985.

Brohom, Richard R. "How Can You Believe You're a Minister When the Church Keeps Telling You You're Not?" In *The Laity in Ministry*. George Peck and John S. Hoffman, eds. Valley Forge, PA: Judson Press, 1984.

Brueggemann, Walter. *Finally Comes the Poet*. Philadelphia: Fortress Press, 1989.

———. *First and Second Samuel*. Interpretation: A Bible Commentary for Teaching and Preaching. Louisville, KY: John Knox, 1990.

———. *Hopeful Imagination: Prophetic Voices in Exile*. Philadelphia: Fortress Press, 1986.

———. *In Man We Trust: The Neglected Side of Biblical Faith*. Richmond, VA: John Knox, 1972.

Bullock, C. Hassell. *An Introduction to the Old Testament Poetic Books*. Chicago: Moody Press, 1988.

Butcher, Andy. "When Christians Quit Church." *Charisma Online* (January 31, 2005). No pages. Online: http://www.charismamag.com/index.php/covers/260-cover-story /10434-when-christians-quit-church-.

Cartledge, Mark J. *Practical Theology: Charismatic and Empirical Perspective*. Waynesboro, GA: Paternoster Press, 2003.

Childress, Kyle. "Ties that Bind: Sharing a Common Rule of Life." *Christian Reflection*. Center for Christian Ethics at Baylor University (2010) 33–40. Online: http://www .baylor.edu/christianethics/index.php?id=75873.

Clinebell, Howard J., Jr. "Experiments in Training Laity for Ministry." *Journal of Pastoral Psychology* 22, no. 6 (1971) 35–43.

Collins, John N. "Fitting Lay Ministries into a Theology of Ministry: Responding to an American Consensus." *Worship* 79, no. 2 (March 2005) 152–67.

Cooper, C. Burton. "The Disabled God." *Theology Today* 49 (July 1992) 173–82.

Daniel, Lillian. *Tell It Like It Is: Reclaiming the Practice of Testimony*. Herndon, VA: Alban Institute, 2005.

Dart, John. "Oldline Protestant Churches Feeling Their Age." *Christianity Today* (October 6, 2009) 12–13.

DeMerode, Marie. "Theology of the Laity Today." *Lumen Vitae* (1987) 140–53.

Drakeford, John W. *Integrity Therapy*. Nashville: Broadman Press, 1967.

Dusing, Michael. "'Trophimus Have I Left at Miletus Sick'—The Case for Those Who Are Not Healed," Thirty-first Annual Meeting of the Society for Pentecostal Studies Southeastern University, Lakeland, Florida. March 14–16, 2002.

Dykstra, Craig. "Imagination and the Pastoral Life: A Way of Seeing." *Christian Century* (April 8, 2008) 26–31.

Edge, Findley B. "Faith and Mission: God's Call to the Laity." *Faith and Mission* 1, no. 1 (1983) 15–27.

Eichrodt, Walter. *Theology of the Old Testament*. 2 vols. Philadelphia: Westminster Press, 1961.

Eisland, Nancy. "Encountering the Disabled God." *The Other Side* (2002) 10–15.

Ellington, Scott. "The Costly Loss of Testimony." *Journal for Pentecostal Theology* 16 (2000) 48–59.

———. "History, Story, and Testimony: Locating Truth in a Pentecostal Hermeneutic." *Pneuma* 23 (Fall 2001) 245–63.

Elmer, Duane. *Cross-Cultural Servanthood: Serving the World in Christ-like Humility*. Downers Grove, IL: InterVarsity, 2006.

Fenhagen, James C. *Mutual Ministry*. San Francisco: Harper Row, 1997.

Fettke, Steven M. "Ministers According to God's Purpose: The Role of the Laity in Ministry," Twenty-first Annual Meeting of the Society for Pentecostal Studies,

Southeastern College of the Assemblies of God, Lakeland, Florida. November 7–9, 1991.

———. "The Spirit of God Hovered Over the Waters: Creation, the local Church, and the Mentally and Physically Challenged, A Call to Spirit-led Ministry." *Journal for Pentecostal Theology* 17, no. 2 (November 2, 2008) 170–82.

Fortin, Jack. "The Centered Life Initiative: Equipping the Saints." *Word & Word* 25, no. 4 (Fall 2005) 363–72.

Furnish, Victor Paul. "Theology and Ministry in the Pauline Letters" in *A Biblical Basis for Ministry*, Earl Shelp and Ronald Sunderland, eds. Philadelphia: Westminster Press, 1981.

The General Council of the Assemblies of God. "Our 16 Fundamental Truths." No Pages. Online: http://ag.org/top/Beliefs/Statement_of_Fundamental_Truths/sft_full.cfm#10.

Gibbs, Eddie. *ChurchNext: Quantum Changes in How We Do Ministry*. Downers Grove, IL: InterVarsity Press, 2000.

Gire, Ken. *Windows of the Soul*. Grand Rapids: Zondervan, 1996.

Hahn, Celia A. *Lay Voices in an Open Church*. Washington, DC: Alban Institute, 1985.

Hall, Douglas John. *When You Pray: Thinking Your Way into God's World*. Valley Forge, PA: Judson Press, 1987.

Hare, Douglas R. A. *Matthew*. Interpretation: A Bible Commentary for Teaching and Preaching. Atlanta: Westminster/John Knox, 1993.

Harrison, R. K. *Introduction to the Old Testament*. Grand Rapids: Wm. B. Eerdmans, 1969.

Hauerwas, Stanley, and Jean Vanier. *Living Gently in a Violent World: The Prophetic Witness of Weakness*. Downers Grove, IL: InterVarsity Press, 2008.

Hays, Richard. *First Corinthians*. Interpretation: A Bible Commentary for Teaching and Preaching. Atlanta: Westminster/John Knox, 1997.

Henn, William. "The Identity and Mission of the Laity from the Point of View of Ecclesiology." *Studia Missionalia* 49 (2000) 83–118.

Hesselgrave, Douglas J. *Communicating Christ Cross-Culturally: An Introduction to Missionary Communication*. Grand Rapids: Zondervan, 1991.

Hodges, Melvin. *A Theology of the Church and Its Mission: A Pentecostal Perspective*. Springfield, MO: Gospel Publishing House, 1977.

Holmes, Arthur. *All Truth Is God's Truth*. Grand Rapids: Wm. B. Eerdmans, 1977.

Hull, John M. "The Broken Body in a Broken World: A Contribution to a Christian Doctrine of the Person from a Disabled Point of View." *Journal of Religion, Disability and Heath* 7, no. 4 (2003).

Jeffery, Paul. "Short-term Mission Trips: Beyond Good Intentions." *Christian Century* (December 12, 2001) 5–7.

Johnson, C. Neal. *Business as Mission: A Comprehensive Guide to Theory and Practice*. Downers Grove, IL: InterVarsity Press, 2009.

Jones, L. Gregory. "You're Lonely, I'm Lonely." *Christian Century* (January 26, 2010) 35.

Kanagaraj, Jey J. "The Involvement of the Laity in the Ministry of the Church." *Journal of Evangelical Review of Theology* 21, no. 4 (1997) 326–31.

Karkkainen, Veli-Matti. "Spirit, Laity, Ministry" in *Toward a Pneumatological Theology*. Amos Yong, ed. Lanham, MD: University Press of America, 2002.

Kauffman, Ivan J. "Evangelicals and Monastics." *Christian Reflection*. Center for Christian Ethics at Baylor University (2010) 26–32. Online: http://www.baylor.edu/christianethics/index.php?id=75873

Kerr, J. R. "Open Source Activists." *Leadershipjournal.net* (October 1, 2009). No Pages. Online: http://www.christianitytoday.com/le/2009/summer/opensourceactivists. html.

Kimball, Dan. *They Like Jesus But Not the Church: Insights from Emerging Generations.* Grand Rapids: Zondervan, 2007.

Kingsolver, Barbara. *The Poisonwood Bible.* San Francisco: Harper, 2008.

Kirk, J. Andrew. "Sundry Thoughts on Lay Ministry in a Fast-changing World." *Studia Missionalia Journal* 49 (2000) 345–62.

Kraemer, Hendrik. *Theology of the Laity.* Philadelphia: Westminster Press, 1958.

Leonard, Bill J. "The Church and the Laity." *Review and Expositor* 85, no. 4 (1988) 625–35.

Lingenfelter, Sherwood G., and Marvin K. Mayers. *Ministering Cross-Culturally: An Incarnational Model for Personal Relationships.* Grand Rapids: Baker, 1986.

Long, Thomas G. "Preaching in the Middle of a Saintly Conversation." *Journal for Preachers* 18, no. 2 (Lent 1995) 15–21.

———. "Struggling Toward Ash Wednesday: Preaching Epiphany at the Beginning of the New Millenium." *Journal for Preachers* 23 (Advent 1999) 25–31.

———. *Testimony: Talking Ourselves into Being Christian.* San Francisco: Josey Bass, 2004.

Luther, Martin. *Lectures on Galatians.* Luther's Works, vol. 27. Philadelphia: Fortress Press, 1957.

Macchia, Frank D. "A Reply to Rickie Moore." *Journal for Pentecostal Theology* 17 (October 2000) 15–19.

———. "Signs of Grace in a Graceless World: Toward a Spirit-Baptized Ecclesiology" in *Baptized in the Spirit: A Global Pentecostal Theology.* Grand Rapids: Zondervan, 2006.

———. "The Struggle for the Spirit in The Church: The Gifts of the Spirit and the Kingdom of God in Pentecostal Perspective." *Theology and Worship Tidings* 10 (2000) 16–17.

MacDonald, Gordon. "Incarnate Preaching." *Leadershipjournal.net* (July 7, 2007). No Pages. Online: http://www.christianitytoday.com/le/2007 /summer/14.48.html.

MacDougal, Carolyn. "Ministry in the Work Setting: A Personal Study." In *The Laity in Ministry.* George Peck and John S. Hoffmann, eds. Valley Forge, PA: Judson Press, 1984.

MacIlvaine, W. Rodman, III. "How Churches Become Missional." *Bibliotheca Sacra* 167 (April-June 2010) 216–33.

Mannion, Gerard. "New Wine and New Wineskins: Laity and a Liberative Future for the Church." *International Journal of Practical Theology* 11, no. 2 (2007) 193–211.

Marney, Carlyle. *Priests to Each Other.* Valley Forge, PA: Judson Press, 1974.

Martens, Elmer A. *God's Design: A Focus on Old Testament Theology.* Grand Rapids: Baker, 1981.

McKnight, Scot. "Jesus Creed: What is the Focus of Spiritual Life?" *Christian Century* (September 7, 2004) 22–24.

McQuilkin, Robertson. "Muriel's Blessing." *Christianity Today* (February 1, 2004). Online: http://www.ctlibrary.com/ct/2004/februaryweb-only/2-9-12.0.html.

Michener, James. *Hawaii: A Novel.* New York: Random House, 2002.

Miller, Edward Jeremy. "Newman on the Voice of the Laity: Lessons for Today's Church." *Newman Studies Journal* 3, no. 2 (2006) 16–31.

Moltmann, Jurgen. *The Church in the Power of the Spirit: A Contribution to Messianic Ecclesiology.* New York: Harper and Row, 1977.

Moore, Mary Elizabeth. "Commissioning the People of God: Called to Be a Community in Missions." *Journal of Quarterly Review* 23, no. 4 (2003) 399–411.

Murphy, Roland. *Wisdom Literature and Psalms*. Nashville: Abingdon Press, 1983.

Neill, Stephen Charles, and Hans-Ruedi Weber. *The Layman in Christian History*. Philadelphia: Westminster Press, 1963.

Nelson, C. Ellis. *How Faith Matures*. Louisville, KY: Westminster/John Knox, 1989.

Nerken, Ira. "Making It Safe to Grieve." *Christian Century* (November 30, 1988) 1091–94.

Newbigin, Leslie. *The Household of God*. London: SCM Press, 1953.

Norris, Kathleen. *The Cloister Walk*. New York: Riverhead Books, 1996.

Nouwen, Henri. *Turn My Mourning into Dancing: Finding Hope in Hard Times*. Nashville: Thomas Nelson, 2004.

———. *The Wounded Healer*. New York: Bantam, Doubleday, Dell, 1979.

O'Brien, Oonagh. "The Theology of Lay Ministry: Developments Since Vatican II." *Irish Theological Quarterly* 72, no. 1 (2007) 88–95.

Palma, Anthony D. "Who is a Minister?" *Advance* (1979) 12–13.

Palmer, Parker. "Now I Become Myself." *Yesmagazine.org* (Spring 2001). No Pages. Online: http://www.yesmagazine.org/issues/working-for-life/now-i-become-myself.

Paulsell, Stephanie. "Body Language: Clothing Ourselves and Others." *Christian Century* (January 16–23, 2002) 18–24.

Peterson, Eugene H. *The Contemplative Pastor: Returning to the Art of Spiritual Direction*. Grand Rapids: Wm. B. Eerdmans, 1989.

———. *Five Smooth Stones for Pastoral Work*. Grand Rapids: Wm. B. Eerdmans, 1980.

———. *Under the Predictable Plant: An Exploration in Vocational Holiness*. Grand Rapids: Wm. B. Eerdmans, 1992.

———. *Where Your Treasure Is: Psalms that Summon You from Self to Community*. Grand Rapids: Wm. B. Eerdmans, 1989.

Phillips, Wallace. *All Dressed Up and No Place to Go: Closed Doors at the Lord's House*. Greensboro, NC: Diakonia Publishing, 2007.

Polischuk, Pablo. "The Caring Church: Training Laity for Pastoral Care and Counseling." *Enrichment* 15, no. 3 (Summer 2010) 66–71.

Poloma, Margaret. *The Assemblies of God at the Crossroads: Charisma and Institutional Dilemmas*. Knoxville: University of Tennessee Press, 1989.

———. "Charisma and Institution: The Assemblies of God." *Christian Century* (October 17, 1990) 932–34.

Radecke, Mark Wm. "Misguided Missions: Ten Worst Practices." *Christian Century* (May 18, 2010) 22–25.

Robeck, Cecil M., Jr. *The Azusa Street Mission and Revival: The Birth of the Global Pentecostal Movement*. Nashville: Thomas Nelson, 2006.

Robinson, H. Wheeler. *Inspiration and Revelation in the Old Testament*. Oxford: Clarendon Press, 1946.

Robinson, Martin, and Dwight Smith. *Invading Secular Space: Strategies for Tomorrow's Church*. Grand Rapids: Monarch Books, 2003.

Russell, Letty M. *Just Hospitality: God's Welcome in a World of Difference*. J. Shannon Clarkson and Kate M. Ott, eds. Atlanta: Westminster/John Knox, 2009.

Smith, Donald P. "Shared Ministry." *Theology Today* 36, no. 3 (Fall 1979) 338–46.

Smith, Frank. *To Think*. New York: Columbia University Press, 1991.

Steffen, Tom, and Lois McKinney Douglas. *Encountering Missionary Life and Work: Preparing for Intercultural Ministry*. Grand Rapids: Baker, 2008.

Stevens, R. Paul. *Liberating the Laity: Equipping All the Saints for Ministry*. Downers Grove, IL: InterVarsity Press, 1985.

Stockard, Jim. "Commissioning the Ministries of the Laity: How It Works and Why It Isn't Being Done." In *The Laity in Ministry*. George Peck and John S. Hoffmann, eds. Valley Forge, PA: Judson Press, 1984.

Swenson, Kristin. "Biblically Challenged: Overcoming Spiritual Illiteracy." *ChristianCentury* (November 3, 2009) 22–25.

Tanksley, Perry. *I Call You Friend*. Jackson, MS: Allgood Books, 1972.

Taylor, Brian C. "Changing Your Mind: Contemplative Prayer and Personal Transformative." *Sewanee Theological Review* 48, no. 2 (Easter 2005) 182–97.

Thornburgh, Ginny, ed. *That All May Worship*. Washington, DC: National Organization on Disability, 1993.

Tinlin, Paul B., and Edith Blumhofer. "Decade of Decline or Harvest? Dilemmas of the Assemblies of God." *Christian Century* (July 10–17, 1991) 684–87.

Tolstoy, Leo. *Walk in the Light and Twenty-Three Tales*. Maryknoll, NY: Orbis, 2003.

Volf, Miroslav. *After Our Likeness: The Church as the Image of the Trinity*. Grand Rapids: Wm. B. Eerdmans, 1998.

Vos, Nelvin. "Laity in the World: The Church at Work." *Journal of Word & World* 4, no. 2 (1984) 151–58.

Ward, Angie. "Discerning Your Church's Hidden Core Values." *Leadershipjournal .net* (January 17, 2005). No Pages. Online: http://www.christianitytoday.com/le /currenttrendscolumns/leadershipweekly/cln50117.html?start=1.

Wheeler, Barbara. "Ready to Lead? The Problems with Lay Pastors." *Christian Century* (July 13, 2010) 28–33.

Whitney-Brown, Carolyn. *Jean Vanier: Essential Writings* in *Modern Spiritual Masters Series*. Robert Ellsberg, ed. Maryknoll, NY: Orbis, 2008.

Wilson-Hartgrove, Johnathan. "A Vision so Old it Looks New." *Christian Reflection*. Center for Christian Ethics at Baylor University (2010) 11–18. Online: http://www .baylor.edu/christianethics/index.php?id=75873

Wood, Lawrence. "Called but Not Ordained: The Need for Lay Pastors." *Christian Century* (July 13, 2010) 22–27.

Worley, Robert C. *A Gathering of Strangers*. Philadelphia: Westminster Press, 1984.

Yong, Amos. "The Acts of the Apostles and of the Holy Spirit: Toward a Pneumatological Ecclesiology" in *The Spirit Poured Out On All Flesh: Pentecostalism and the Possibility of a Global Theology*. Grand Rapids: Baker Academic, 2005.

———. *Hospitality and the Other: Pentecost, Christian Practices, and the Neighbor*. New York: Orbis, 2008.

———. "Many Tongues, Many Senses: Pentecost, the Body Politic, and the Redemption of Dis/Ability." *Pneuma* 31, no. 2 (2009) 167–88.

———. *Theology and Down Syndrome: Reimagining Disability in Late Modernity*. Waco, TX: Baylor University Press, 2007.

Subject/Name Index